5/23

D0484942

MYSTERY
OF THE
KINGDOM

On the Gospel of Matthew

Edward P. Sri

EMMAUS
ROAD
PUBLISHING

*Dedicated to
my father and mother,
Prasit and Antoinette Sri,
with love and gratitude.*

MYSTERY OF THE KINGDOM

On the Gospel of Matthew

Edward P. Sri

EMMAUS
ROAD
PUBLISHING

Unless otherwise indicated, Scripture quotations are
taken from the Revised Standard Version, Catholic
Edition (RSVCE), copyright © 1965 and 1966 by the
Division of Christian Education of the National Council
of the Churches of Christ in the United States of
America. Used by permission.

Excerpts from the English translation of the *Catechism of
the Catholic Church* for the United States of America
copyright © 1994, United States Catholic Conference—
Libreria Editrice Vaticana. All rights reserved.

Nihil Obstat
Rev. James Dunfee
Censor Librorum

Imprimatur ✠
Most Rev. Gilbert I. Sheldon, D.D., D.Min.

Copyright © 1999
Emmaus Road Publishing
All rights reserved.

Library of Congress catalog no. 00-100215

Published by
Emmaus Road Publishing
827 North Fourth Street
Steubenville, Ohio 43952
1-800-398-5470

On the Cover
Christ Delivering the Keys to St. Peter (detail) /Perugino

Cover design and layout by
Beth Hart

Published in the United States of America
ISBN 0-9663223-5-5

CONTENTS

ABBREVIATIONS

The Old Testament
Gen./Genesis
Ex./Exodus
Lev./Leviticus
Num./Numbers
Deut./Deuteronomy
Josh./Joshua
Judg./Judges
Ruth/Ruth
1 Sam./1 Samuel
2 Sam./2 Samuel
1 Kings/1 Kings
2 Kings/2 Kings
1 Chron./1 Chronicles
2 Chron./2 Chronicles
Ezra/Ezra
Neh./Nehemiah
Tob./Tobit
Jud./Judith
Esther/Esther
Job/Job
Ps./Psalms
Prov./Proverbs
Eccles./Ecclesiastcs
Song/Song of Solomon
Wis./Wisdom
Sir./Sirach (Ecclesiasticus)
Is./Isaiah
Jer./Jeremiah
Lam./Lamentations
Bar./Baruch
Ezek./Ezekiel
Dan./Daniel
Hos./Hosea

Joel/Joel
Amos/Amos
Obad./Obadiah
Jon./Jonah
Mic./Micah
Nahum/Nahum
Hab./Habakkuk
Zeph./Zephaniah
Hag./Haggai
Zech./Zechariah
Mal./Malachi
1 Mac./1 Maccabees
2 Mac./2 Maccabees

The New Testament
Mt./Matthew
Mk./Mark
Lk./Luke
Jn./John
Acts/Acts of the Apostles
Rom./Romans
1 Cor./1 Corinthians
2 Cor./2 Corinthians
Gal./Galatians
Eph./Ephesians
Phil./Philippians
Col./Colossians
1 Thess./1 Thessalonians
2 Thess./2 Thessalonians
1 Tim./1 Timothy
2 Tim./2 Timothy
Tit./Titus
Philem./Philemon

Heb./Hebrews
Jas./James
1 Pet./1 Peter
2 Pet./2 Peter
1 Jn./1 John
2 Jn./2 John
3 Jn./3 John
Jude/Jude
Rev./Revelation (Apocalypse)

Catechism of the Catholic Church

Throughout the text, the *Catechism of the Catholic Church* (United States Catholic Conference–Libreria Editrice Vaticana, 1994, as revised in the 1997 Latin typical edition) will be cited simply as "Catechism."

FOREWORD

Christians today have acquired some peculiar habits in the way we read the Gospels. Some of us buy little editions of the New Testament all by itself. Some translations render the texts in an idiom that reads almost like modern street speech.

If these conveniences make the Gospels accessible to more people, I applaud them. But we should also recognize that they bring along certain limitations. The stand-alone New Testaments, for example, can condition readers to dissociate the New from the Old Testament and lose the thread of continuity that runs through all of salvation history. The modern idiom, for its part, can sometimes drain the Gospel of its Israelite blood, its "Jewishness." The unfortunate result is that some people come to see salvation as something that arose, almost out of nowhere, as an essentially American phenomenon.

We should all be grateful, then, to Edward Sri for writing *Mystery of the Kingdom: On the Gospel of Matthew*. This book restores the Gospel that too often gets lost in the translation. For to drain the Jewishness from Matthew is to drain the life from its pages. These opening pages of the New Testament concern themselves with the fulfillment of Israel's messianic hopes, that a Son of David would come to establish a kingdom that would last forever.

We cannot understand the first Gospel if we do not understand precisely what its author meant by the *kingdom of heaven*. Some people look at the kingdom in a deistic way: God exercising His rule in governance of every square inch of the universe. Yet this has always been true, before and after the Fall, before and after the coming of the Messiah. No, the kingdom of God means something more. For Matthew and for Jesus, the kingdom is the specific form God's covenant took: first, imperfectly, with King David and later, in a perfect way, with His ultimate and everlasting heir, Jesus Christ.

In this study of Matthew, we see a sublime demonstration of Saint Augustine's principle for understanding the Scriptures: the New Testament is concealed in the Old, and the Old is revealed in the New. For the kingdom, in the New Testament as in the Old, takes a concrete form: in the New Testament, it is the Church.

This resolves an otherwise insoluble problem. As the apostate scholar Alfred Loisy put it: Jesus came promising the kingdom, but all He left us was the Church. Edward Sri and Saint Matthew show us that what Jesus promised and what He delivered are one and the same. In the words of the Second Vatican Council:

> To carry out the will of the Father Christ inaugurated the kingdom of heaven on earth and revealed to us his mystery; by his obedience he brought about our redemption. The Church—that is, the kingdom of Christ already present in mystery—grows visibly through the power of God in the world (*Lumen Gentium*, no. 3).

Cardinal Christoph Schönborn has commented on this passage: "Thus there lies no distance between

the Church and the kingdom of God."[1] The kingdom
is where the King is present; where the Eucharist is,
there is the King.

What awaits the reader is the discovery of what
made the Gospel so exciting for the first Christians:
that the universal reign has arrived, and it has taken
a specific form. The kingdom of a new Israel, a new
Jerusalem, now extends to all nations. The Old
Covenant has been fulfilled not by replacement, but
by renewal and extension. What Solomon could not
accomplish through his seven hundred strategic mar-
riages to foreign and domestic noblewomen, Christ
accomplished through His one marriage to the
Church.

Edward Sri has moved us beyond the typical modern limitations in reading Matthew. Read this book
attentively, then, and you'll come to a deeper love of
the people and the religion of Israel, the people and
the religion of our Messiah and King.

Scott Hahn

Steubenville, Ohio

---

[1] Cristoph Schönborn, *From Death to Life: The Christian Journey*
(San Francisco: Ignatius Press, 1988), 81-82.

INTRODUCTION

Much has been said about why Jesus died. This book, however, will focus on why Jesus lived.

While the death and Resurrection stand out as the most crucial chapters in the story of Jesus, Our Lord certainly did a lot more with His life than offer it up on the Cross. In fact, we won't be able to fully appreciate the meaning of His death on Good Friday until we understand the mission that Jesus had for His life in the years that went before.

The Gospels tell us many important things about Jesus which occurred long before His Crucifixion on Calvary. First, we know that Jesus became a famous teacher who quickly won the hearts and respect of many of the Jewish people. We also know that Jesus was renowned for His powerful actions of curing the sick, raising the dead, giving sight to the blind, and expelling evil spirits. With His popularity rapidly skyrocketing, large crowds began to follow Him from town to town. Some people gave up everything to become His close associates. Many went so far as to claim Him as their king, pinning their hopes on Him as the one who would bring Israel's history to its ultimate destination and its moment of glory.

At the same time His fame was spreading, Jesus was also known for being somewhat of a troublemaker. His teachings stirred up great controversy, and He faced fierce opposition from the religious leaders of the day. Many of His public actions were considered out of line with traditional Jewish piety.

Even His private social life was under intense
scrutiny: In the eyes of some, Jesus was hanging out
with all the wrong people—the sinners, lepers,
drunkards, and other outcasts with whom most pious
Jews would not want to be closely associated. At the
same time, Jesus frequently challenged the ideolo-
gies and practices of many Jewish leaders, exposing
their hypocrisy and subverting their very authority.
He even went after Israel's most sacred symbol, the
Temple, as He stormed into this holiest of buildings
and turned the place upside down, flipping over
tables and predicting the Temple's imminent
destruction. Actions such as these weren't the best
way to win friends and influence people in first-
century Judaism. In fact, they won for Him many
enemies and ultimately cost Him His life.

So who did Jesus think He was? And why did
Jesus do the things He did? These are the questions
which not only will help us understand the meaning
of Jesus' life, but will also shed light on the meaning
of His death and Resurrection. We can't fully comprehend the last chapters of the story of Jesus unless
we first grasp the meaning of the story that went
before. In other words, we can't fully appreciate why
Jesus died until we understand why He lived.

Jesus' life is like a mosaic. As an ancient form of
religious art, a mosaic is a collection of small pieces
of colored stones or tile cemented on a flat surface in
such a way that, when all the pieces are viewed
together, they form a larger picture. However, if each
colored stone is looked at individually, isolated from
the other stones, the larger image will be missed. To
gaze upon a mosaic, one must step back and look at

the picture as a whole in order to see how all the pieces fit together to form one beautiful work of art. In a similar way, we can know all the bits and pieces of Jesus' ministry, but if we do not know how they fit together, we will miss the larger picture and not understand the purpose of His life. This book is meant to help us step back and look at how all His words and actions actually fit together into one overarching plan. At the center of that plan is Jesus' mission to build the kingdom of heaven on earth.

As we'll see in subsequent chapters of this book, Jesus considered Himself to be Israel's long-awaited king—the prophesied "anointed one," or "messiah"—who would bring God's plan for Israel to fulfillment and empower Israel to be what it was always meant to be. This mission of building His kingdom was at the center of His teachings and at the heart of all His actions. So whether we're considering His great sermons, His parables, and His confrontations with the Pharisees, or we're reading about His Baptism at the Jordan, His temptations in the desert, and His healing the sick, we need to see that all the little pieces of Jesus' life are strategic parts of His kingdom-building plan.

This book will assist the reader in a study of Christ's life and mission as seen through the lenses of Saint Matthew's Gospel. Pope John Paul II once called Matthew "the catechist's Gospel"—perhaps because Matthew, more than the other Gospels, brings together most explicitly this central theme of Jesus' mission, the building of the kingdom. This, of course, has tremendous value not only for under-standing Jesus' life, but also for seeing how Jesus

continues to carry out His mission today through
His kingdom, the Church. Indeed, Catholic readers
will find this Gospel particularly helpful for training
in Catholic doctrine and in understanding the
Church as the kingdom of God. At the same time,
readers from all faith backgrounds will gain a greater
understanding of Jesus' mission in Israel some two
thousand years ago and find some practical insights
into how His kingdom can be lived out in our own
lives today.

Each chapter of this study will offer biblical
reflections on particular sections of Matthew's
Gospel, beginning with Jesus' genealogy in Matthew
1 all the way through Jesus' death and Resurrection
in Matthew 27-28. These reflections attempt to
place Jesus in His first-century Jewish setting and
consider what Jesus' words and actions would have
meant in their original context. Here I will build upon
some of the exciting insights from the recent wave of
historical research into the life and mission of Jesus.
When Jesus is understood in His historical context,
we will see more clearly that practically every move
He made is charged with great meaning and sheds
light on His overall plan to build His kingdom.

Each chapter ends with some questions for group
discussion or private reflection. These questions are
intended to help readers interact directly with the
texts from Saint Matthew's Gospel and experience
the joys of discovering rich insights in the inspired
words of Scripture. There is nothing like reading and
praying through the Gospels and allowing the Lord to
speak to us through the sacred texts! That is why the
questions are also meant to help stimulate thought

and discussion on how Christ can build His kingdom in our own lives today—in our world, in our work, in our families and, most of all, in our own hearts. In closing, I wish to extend my gratitude to the people who have contributed to making this project possible. At Emmaus Road, thanks goes to Leon Suprenant, Beth Hart, Ann Recznik, Jody Trupiano, and Brian Germann for their perseverance in bringing this work to its completion, and to Tim Gray for his wise editorial insights and scholarly inspiration. Curtis Mitch deserves a special note of gratitude for his exegetical precision and our countless conversations, a number of which have left their impression on the pages of this book. Thanksgiving also goes to my students and colleagues at Benedictine College and in the Fellowship Of Catholic University Students (FOCUS), who have been so much a part of this book through their heartfelt interest, enthusiasm, and prayers. Most of all, I thank my dear wife and "final editor," Elizabeth, for her insights as well as her patience, encouragement, and love throughout the past year.

Edward P. Sri
Benedictine College
First Sunday of Advent 1999

JESUS' FAMILY TREE
—MATTHEW 1-2—

For most readers of the Bible, reading a genealogy is about as exciting as reading a telephone book. Yet this is exactly how the entire New Testament begins in chapter one of Saint Matthew's Gospel:

> The book of the genealogy of Jesus Christ, the son of David, the son of Abraham. Abraham was the father of Isaac, and Isaac the father of Jacob, and Jacob the father of Judah and his brothers, and Judah the father of Perez and Zerah . . . (Mt. 1:1-3).

I would bet that many readers today do what I did when I first looked at chapter 1 of this Gospel: skip the genealogy and pick up again in chapter 2. Even the few brave readers who survive the list of forty-two generations are nevertheless probably left wondering, "Couldn't Matthew have chosen a better way to begin his Gospel?" Admittedly, being hit with a family tree of people who lived thousands of years ago doesn't seem to be the most attractive way to lure people into the story of Jesus Christ. As one New Testament scholar put it, "Let's face it: Other people's family trees are about as interesting as other people's holiday videos."[1]

For a Jew in Jesus' day, however, this genealogy would have had more attention-grabbing power than the cover of *Time* magazine or the front page of *U.S.A.*

---

[1] N.T. Wright, *Following Jesus: Biblical Reflections on Discipleship* (Grand Rapids: Eerdmans, 1995), 23.

Today. It would have summed up all their hopes and expectations about what God had been promising to do in their lives ever since the time of Abraham. And it would have triumphantly announced that God's plan had come to completion in their own lifetime! In fact, if there were CNN in first-century Palestine, this little genealogy would have made the top story on "Headline News."

Let's look at Matthew's genealogy with new eyes—with the eyes of first-century Jews who would have seen their history and future and very reason for existing summed up in these few verses. In the process, we will begin to see how this story of Jesus, which sums up the story of Israel, has become our story—the story of the Church.

The Promised "Son of David"

While many people are mentioned in this genealogy, the figure that stands out most is David. It is significant that the first title Matthew bestows on Jesus is the "son of David" (1:1). Another link between David and Jesus is that they are the only individuals who are given titles.[2] David is described as "the king" (1:6) and Jesus is called the "Christ"—meaning "anointed one" (1:16)—a title given to a Davidic king when he was anointed at his coronation. Scholars have also found Davidic imagery in verse 17, in which Matthew draws attention to the number of generations in the genealogy from Abraham to Jesus:

---

[2] On these points, I am indebted to my friend and colleague Curtis Mitch, researcher and writer for the forthcoming Ignatius Study Bible.

[T]he generations from Abraham to David were fourteen generations, and from David to the deportation to Babylon fourteen generations, and from the deportation to Babylon to the Christ fourteen generations (Mt. 1:17).

Matthew divides the generations into three sets of fourteen. He is drawing our attention to the number fourteen, which is significant because David's name adds up to fourteen in Hebrew. Let me explain. In the Hebrew alphabet, consonants are also given numeric value. They represent not only letters, but also numbers. The three Hebrew consonants in David's name are dwd (d = 4, w = 6), adding up to fourteen. Thus, the very structure of Matthew's genealogy centered around three sets of fourteen generations subtly proclaims Jesus to be the "thrice-Davidic Son of David."[3] Interestingly, David himself appears as the 14th generation in the family tree of Saint Matthew's Gospel.

Why all this focus on David? Allusions to David would bring to mind the glory days of Israel's history, when the kingdom reached its peak in terms of its political and religious power and influence in the world. God promised David and his descendants an everlasting dynasty: "[Y]our house and your kingdom shall be made sure for ever before me; your throne shall be established for ever" (2 Sam. 7:16). This dynasty would have worldwide influence. The

---

[3] Marshall D. Johnson, *The Purpose of the Biblical Genealogies, with Special References to the Setting of the Genealogies of Jesus* (Society for New Testament Studies, Monograph Series, 8; London: Cambridge University, 1969), 192.

Davidic king would rule over all the earth, nations would bow down before him, and in him all peoples would find blessing (cf. Ps. 2:8; 72:8-11, 17; 110:6).

One can imagine the excitement a Jew would have felt in reading about the great King David in this genealogy. In the preamble to the genealogy, Jesus is identified as a "son of David." Then the genealogy traces the descendants of Abraham down to "David the king" (Mt. 1:6) and goes on to list the kings of Judah flowing from David's line (Mt. 1:7-10).

The Fallen Kingdom

But then in verse 11 comes a major turning point in the genealogy which issues a somber note for Jewish readers—a sudden, sharp minor chord in the genealogy's triumphant march through David's royal descendants: "and Josiah the father of Jechoniah and his brothers, *at the time of the deportation to Babylon.*" Here, Matthew highlights the Babylonian deportation not so much as a chronological marker, but as a sign-post signaling a tragic shift in the story of Israel: the end of the Davidic monarchy. These words would recall how all of Israel's hopes surrounding the dynasty were dashed in 587 B.C. when the Babylonians conquered Jerusalem, destroyed the Temple, and carried off the people and even their king into a most humiliating and painful exile.

Even more, this exile was not simply a painful memory from the distant past, but an abiding reality for the Jews in Jesus' day, who continued to feel the effects of this devastating loss. For practically six centuries following the Babylonian exile, the Jewish people suffered oppression under the hands of various foreign nations up to the time of Jesus, when the Romans ruled the land. For hundreds of years, the Jews were a nation without control over their own land and a people without a true Davidic king.

The end of the kingdom was not simply a political disaster or military defeat. For a long time, God's prophets had been reminding the people that Israel's strength depended not on military might, economic wealth, or political maneuvering, but on covenant faithfulness to the one true God. Israel's law taught them that if they broke their covenant relationship with Yahweh, they would suffer the curse of exile, in which even their king would be carried away by a foreign nation and God would no longer be with them (cf. Deut. 28:32-36; 31:16-18). This is exactly what happened at the time of the deportation to Babylon (cf. 2 Kings 24).

With Matthew's mention of the Babylonian exile, all the sadness, frustration, and despair which surrounded the first-century Jews' experience of suffering and oppression would ring loudly in their ears. The genealogy continues these somber notes and minor chords by listing the next two generations of oppressed Davidic descendants up to Zerubbabel in verse 12.

Christ and the Kingdom's Restoration

Yet God offered the Jews some hope during this period of suffering and exile. He sent His prophets to tell how a new Davidic king would be raised up—a Messiah ("Anointed One") who would restore the kingdom and bring about the New Covenant era in which there would be forgiveness of sins and blessing for the whole world.[4] Many first-century Jews reading Matthew's genealogy would be longing for these promises to be fulfilled.

Matthew plays upon those hopes in verse 13, where the genealogy slowly begins to change keys again. While verse 12 mentions Zerubbabel, who was the last of the Davidic descendants in Matthew's genealogy to be mentioned in the Old Testament, verse 13 offers a sign of new hope, showing how the Davidic royal line continued even after Zerubbabel. This, no doubt, would stir excitement and anticipation: The Davidic line continues! Perhaps we will find the Messiah at the end of this line!

The genealogy builds a hopeful momentum as it introduces each descendent after Zerubbabel—men who were previously unrecorded in Scripture: Abiud, Eliakim, Azor, Zadok, Achim. . . . Finally, it reaches the peak of its crescendo when Matthew presents "Joseph the husband of Mary, of whom Jesus was born, who is called Christ" (1:16). Here, the chorus resounds at the climax of the whole genealogy: Jesus is the "Christ"—the Messiah whom God had foretold would restore the kingdom and bring to completion His plan of bringing blessing to the entire world!

Emmanuel: God with Us

The chorus continues into verses 18-23, in which Matthew highlights two more titles for this great royal Son. First, Matthew shows us how this Child's very name has great importance. He shall be called "Jesus,"

---

[4] See, e.g., Jer. 33:15 *et seq.*; Jer. 23:1-6; Ezek. 34; Amos 9:11-12; Dan. 9:25-26; cf. Is. 45:1-5, 21-25.

which literally means "God saves." Why is He given this name? Matthew tells us through the angel's explanation to Joseph: "[A]nd you shall call his name Jesus, for he will save his people from their sins" (1:21). Here we see that Jesus' name in verse 21 is the answer to the problem of the Babylonian exile in verse 11.[5] Remember, the Jews viewed their exilic condition not simply as a political or military problem, but as a sin problem. According to their prophets and their law, it was covenant unfaithfulness that brought about their exile and oppression. Thus, Jesus ("God saves") comes to "save his people from their sins," thereby saving the Jews from the real exile—which is not being chained down by the Babylonians or Romans, but being enslaved to the real oppressor, the devil, who has a hold over all humanity through the chains of sin and death.

Of all the titles for Jesus that Matthew highlights, perhaps the most profound one comes right at the end of his first chapter. Jesus is called "Emmanuel," which means "God with us" (Mt. 1:23). We cannot understate how much this must have meant to ancient Jews. Ever since the first sin, when Adam and Eve "hid themselves from the presence of the LORD" (Gen. 3:8), God has been working to restore communion with sinful humanity. And God planned to use Israel as His chosen people and the Davidic king as their leader and representative in order to reach the nations and gather all people back into communion with the one true God. But without their kingdom,

---

[5] See John Mark Jones, "Subverting the Textuality of Davidic Messianism: Matthew's Presentation of the Genealogy of the Davidic Title," *Catholic Biblical Quarterly* 56 (1994), 263-64.

without a Davidic king, and still suffering under foreign domination, some first-century Jews might have wondered what happened to God's great promises for their nation and felt somewhat abandoned. Was God still with His people?

But Matthew triumphantly proclaims that the royal Child at the end of the genealogy is the answer to their hearts' deepest longings. Not only is He the Christ—the anointed Davidic king who will restore the kingdom. And not only is He Jesus, the one who will save His people from their sins. He is Emmanuel— God with us. God is with His people again!

Indeed, as we shall see in subsequent reflections on Matthew's Gospel, the New Covenant which Jesus inaugurates restores communion with Our Heavenly Father and gives us God's presence in a way like never before: God is with us in the Church, in His Word, in the sacraments, and most intimately in the Holy Eucharist. If you want to see just how important this theme of "Emmanuel" is for Saint Matthew, turn to the very end of his Gospel. Just as "God with us" appears as the climactic name for Jesus at the end of Matthew 1, so it appears at the culmination of Matthew's entire Gospel in Jesus' last words to the apostles, promising them that He will be with them always, even to the end of time:

> Go therefore and make disciples of all nations, baptizing them in the name of the Father and of the Son and of the Holy Spirit, teaching them to observe all that I have commanded you; and lo, *I am with you always*, to the close of the age (Mt. 28:19-20).

*   *   *

Questions for Discussion

1. Note how the genealogy in Matthew 1 draws immediate attention to Jesus' being a royal descendant of King David. Let's consider why this would be an important part of Jesus' heritage that Matthew would want to emphasize.

(a) According to the following verses, what promises did God make to David and his descendants?

2 Samuel 7:8-17 _____

Psalm 89:20-37 _____

Psalm 132:11-12 _____

(b) Read Isaiah 11:1-2, 6-12. This prophecy described how the Davidic dynasty was like a strong tree that has been cut off and reduced to a stump when the Babylonians destroyed Jerusalem and carried the people into exile in 587 B.C. In this time of exile, it appeared as if all of the royal descendants of David had been wiped out and the Davidic dynasty had ceased forever. But the prophet Isaiah offered a message a hope: the Davidic line continued! A branch in David's family tree quietly continued to grow out of the stump, and at the end of this branch there will eventually blossom a great king who will restore the kingdom to Israel.

What else did the prophets say about this future son of David who would restore the kingdom? What do the following passages add?

Isaiah 7:14-17 _____

Isaiah 9:2-7 _____

Micah 5:1-4 _____

Ezekiel 34:23-31 _____

Jeremiah 23:1-6 _____

(c) What are the various ways the genealogy in
Matthew 1 draws attention to Jesus' being this long-
awaited Davidic king? Consider the following verses:

Matthew 1:1 _____

Matthew 1:16 _____

Matthew 1:17 _____

Matthew 1:13-16 _____

Other verses and themes in Matthew 1 _____

_____

(d) In light of this background, why would this
genealogy in Matthew 1 grab the first-century Jewish
readers' attention? What would it mean to them?

_____

_____

_____

2. Read 2 Kings 24:10-15. Why might Matthew's mention of the Babylonian exile be considered a somber
note or downward shift in the genealogy?

_____

_____

_____

3. Who was Zerubbabel (Mt. 1:12)? Why would the names listed after him be so important (Mt. 1:13-16)?

_____

_____

4. What is the meaning of Jesus being called the "Christ" ("Messiah") at the end of the genealogy in Matthew 1:16?

_____

_____

5. Read Matthew 1:22-23.

(a) At the end of the first chapter, Jesus is called "Emmanuel." What does this word mean?

_____

(b) Why would this name for Jesus be important to the Jewish people who had been oppressed for over five hundred years?

_____

_____

(c) In what ways does Jesus continue to be with us today? Consider Matthew 18:20 and Matthew 28:16-20.

_____

_____

_____

2

THE KING'S ANOINTING
—MATTHEW 3—

The first time I visited the Jordan River—the place where John the Baptist began his ministry—I couldn't help but think that this prophet could have chosen a much better place to launch his career of preparing the Jewish people for the Messiah.

The Jordan River flows through a barren wilderness into the lowest point on the entire face of the earth, some 1,200 feet below sea level. To get there, the crowds would have to trek several hours down through the rugged desert terrain with the hot, piercing sun relentlessly beating down on their backs. Who would want to go all the way down *there* to hear John the Baptist? It seems that the capital city of Jerusalem would have been a much better site for attracting listeners. Or maybe the densely populated region of Galilee. But the empty wilderness and the Jordan River basin?

Yet, for the ancient Jews, the Jordan River valley was much more than a desolate wilderness. It was the very place where they expected God to do great things for Israel again. And this makes all the difference for understanding the mission of John the Baptist and his fateful encounter with Jesus at that river.

Symbolism of the Jordan River

The Jews knew that great things happened at the Jordan River. This is the place where the prophet Elisha cured Naaman, servant of the King of Syria

(2 Kings 5:1-14). This is where the prophet Elijah was taken up into heaven in a fiery chariot (2 Kings 2:1-10). But most of all, this river would bring to mind the most important event in Israel's history—the Exodus. To this day, Jews annually recall the story of the Exodus, retelling how God freed the Israelites from slavery in Egypt, led them through the Red Sea, and guided them in the desert for forty years. The climax of this drama comes when Joshua led the Israelites through the Jordan River and into the land God had promised them. It was then that Israel began its life anew as a nation in the land of Canaan.

As such, the Jordan River valley became a rich symbol for new beginnings and new life. It expressed Israel's hopes for the future, hopes for a new type of exodus, when God would once again free His people from their pagan enemies as He did back in the time of Moses and Joshua. In fact, the prophets foretold how the desert would be the stage where Israel would return to God and their covenant would be renewed. For example, the prophet Hosea described how sinful Israel would come back to Yahweh like an unfaithful wife returning to her husband. And this spousal reunion would take place in the desert:

> Therefore, behold, I will allure her, and bring her into the wilderness, and speak tenderly to her. . . . And I will make for you a covenant. . . . I will betroth you to me for ever (Hos. 2:14, 18-19).

This is why John the Baptist called the people out into the wilderness to be baptized in the Jordan. Such an action would signal the beginning of all that the Jews had been hoping for. This was a symbolic action, ritually reenacting the Exodus. Just like their ancestors, the Jews following John the Baptist went out into the wilderness, passed through the Jordan, and reentered the Promised Land. And they came out on the other side with all their hopes for a fresh start—hopes for freedom, this time not from the Egyptians but from their current oppressors, the Romans. One can imagine the great enthusiasm and anticipation surrounding John the Baptist's movement. It's no wonder John had little trouble attracting so many people!

Clothes Make the Prophet?

"Now John wore a garment of camel's hair, and a leather girdle around his waist. . ." (Mt. 3:4).

Saint Matthew's Gospel does not tell us much about what John the Baptist taught at the Jordan. In fact, he only quotes nine words from John's actual preaching: "Repent, for the kingdom of heaven is at hand" (Mt. 3:2). It might seem odd that Matthew uses more words describing the type of clothes John the Baptist was wearing than he does telling us about the content of John's message. However, anyone familiar with the Old Testament would find great significance in John's being garbed in camel's hair and a leather girdle around his waist—for this is exactly what the great prophet Elijah was known for wearing (cf. 2 Kings 1:8).

This was significant because the Jews had been waiting for Elijah's return. To understand this, consider the very last prophetic words addressed to Israel in the Old Testament. Malachi was the last prophet sent to Israel and, in his final prophetic utterance, he said Elijah would in some way return to

Israel before the time of the Messiah (cf. Mal. 4:5). For centuries after Malachi, the Jewish people waited in silence with no prophet being sent to them (cf. 1 Mac. 9:27; 14:41). These last words about Elijah's reappearance were left echoing in their ears, as they anticipated the coming of Elijah and the Messiah who would follow after him.

Thus, when John began his ministry dressed with Elijah-styled camel's hair and leather girdle, this signaled to the Jews that he was playing the part of the returned Elijah. Indeed, Jesus Himself later recognized this, saying "For all the prophets and the law prophesied until John; and if you are willing to accept it, he is Elijah who is to come" (Mt. 11:13-14). Acting as the new Elijah, John the Baptist announced that Malachi's prophecy was coming to fulfillment and that the time of the Messiah was just around the corner!

But John and Elijah had much more in common than clothing. Both John and Elijah were great prophets. Both challenged evil kings to change their wicked ways, and both were persecuted for doing so. The most striking parallel is the fact that both John and Elijah prepared the way for prophets with even greater ministries than their own. Before Elijah was taken up to heaven, he gave his successor, Elisha, a double portion of his spirit (2 Kings 2:9, 15), which was the launching pad for Elisha's ministry. Elisha then went on to do even greater things than his predecessor Elijah had done. For example, Elisha miraculously cleansed a leper (2 Kings 5:1-19), raised a child from the dead (2 Kings 4:32-37), and multiplied barley loaves to feed a crowd (2 Kings 4:42-44).

All this, of course, prefigures John the Baptist and

Jesus. When John baptized Jesus, Jesus received the Spirit descending upon Him like a dove, and this event served as the foundation for His public ministry. Jesus then went on to do even greater works than John the Baptist. Like Elisha, Jesus also cleansed lepers (Mt. 8:2-4), raised a child from the dead (Mt. 9:23-25), and multiplied barley loaves to feed the multitudes (Jn. 6:9-14; cf. Mt. 14:15-21; 15:32-38).

What is most significant is the *place* where Elijah passed on his prophetic mission to Elisha: the Jordan River (2 Kings 2:6-14). At the Jordan, Elijah transferred his ministry to his successor, Elisha. It was also there that the new Elijah—John the Baptist—passed the baton to Jesus, who then began His public ministry as the new Elisha.

The Messiah's Arrival

With this background, we can appreciate why John the Baptist would attract such a large following. His baptism ministry at the Jordan instilled hope for a new type of exodus, this time bringing liberation from the Romans. And his appearing like Elijah signaled that Israel's long-awaited Messiah-King was soon to arrive on the scene to lead the people to freedom and restore the kingdom.

Nevertheless, John made it clear that he himself was not the exodus leader. He himself was not the Messiah:

> I baptize you with water for repentance, but he who is coming after me is mightier than I, whose sandals I am not worthy to carry; he will baptize you with the Holy Spirit and with fire (Mt. 3:11).

John viewed himself simply as a predecessor, preparing the way for the Messiah.

But then one day, it happened. The Messiah arrived. "Jesus came forth from Galilee to the Jordan to John, to be baptized by him" (Mt. 3:13). What an amazing encounter that must have been! For John, this meeting meant the culmination of his entire career as the prophet who prepared the people for their king. For Jesus, however, it marked the very beginning of His mission as the Messiah.

Catching the Spirit

Jesus' baptism can be seen as His anointing as king and His inauguration as Israel's Messiah.

The word "messiah" ("anointed one" in Hebrew) was often used in the Old Testament to describe the Davidic king who was anointed with oil as he assumed his royal office. The Jews also used the word "messiah" to designate the future anointed king who would carry out the new exodus and restore the Davidic kingdom.

When Jesus comes to the Jordan to be baptized, something happens which would signal to the careful observer that this event marks the beginning of Jesus' ministry as the hoped-for Messiah:

> [T]he heavens were opened and he saw the Spirit of God descending like a dove, and alighting on him; and lo, a voice from heaven, saying, "This is my beloved Son, with whom I am well pleased" (Mt. 3:16-17).

The Spirit's descending on Jesus calls to mind how the Spirit fell upon the Jewish kings of the Old

Testament when they were anointed. For example, Samuel told Saul that one of the signs that he was truly anointed king was that "the spirit of the LORD will come mightily upon you" (1 Sam. 10:6). Similarly when Samuel anointed David as king, "the Spirit of the LORD came mightily upon David from that day forward" (1 Sam. 16:13).

It is not surprising that the Jewish people expected the future Messiah-King to receive the Spirit in a similar way. In fact, the prophet Isaiah made this very point when he foretold how the messianic son of David would receive the Spirit upon him as a source of wisdom, understanding, counsel, and might (Is. 11:2). So the Spirit's coming upon Jesus at the Jordan could be seen as a royal event recalling the anointing of Israel's great kings, including the Messiah.

Anointed Servant

The voice from heaven saying, "This is my beloved Son, with whom I am well pleased" (Mt. 3:17), also has messianic overtones. These words bring to mind an important figure in the Book of Isaiah: the Servant of the Lord, who in some Jewish circles was associated with Israel's hopes for the Messiah.[1]

Isaiah foretold how God would send this Servant to suffer for Israel's sins and bring about the blessings of the New Covenant (Is. 40-55). God would send His

---

[1] Some Jews seem to have interpreted the servant figure in a messianic sense. For example, Zechariah 3:8 describes the messianic "branch" figure (cf. Is. 11:1; Jer. 23:5; 33:15) as "my servant." For further commentary, see N.T. Wright, *Jesus and the Victory of God* (Minneapolis: Fortress Press, 1996), 588-90.

Spirit upon His Servant and rejoice in Him: "Behold my servant . . . in whom my soul delights; I have put my Spirit upon him" (Is. 42:1). In Matthew 3, the voice from heaven draws from this language of Isaiah, showing how Isaiah's prophecy is fulfilled in Jesus' baptism, when the Spirit descends upon Him and the Father declares that He is "well pleased" in Him (Mt. 3:17).

What is significant for our purposes is to see that this coming of the Spirit upon Jesus is Jesus' anointing. Isaiah himself specifically described the Servant's reception of the Spirit as an anointing: "The Spirit of the LORD GOD is upon me, because the LORD has anointed me" (Is. 61:1).[2] And this is how Peter eventually interpreted Jesus' baptism, saying "God anointed Jesus of Nazareth with the Holy Spirit and with power" (Acts 10:38).

Thus, when Jesus comes out of the Jordan, He comes out as Israel's royal Messiah-King anointed by the Holy Spirit (cf. Catechism, no. 535). Now as the truly "Anointed One," Jesus is ready to begin His messianic mission of building the kingdom. Here we can see that the Jordan River in the wilderness certainly was a place of new beginnings!

*   *   *

---

[2] See Donald Hagner, Matthew 1-13 in *Word Biblical Commentary*, vol. 33a (Dallas: Word Books, 1993), 58; Timothy Gray, "Holy Oil in the Desert: The Baptism and Anointing of Jesus" *Lay Witness* (September 1998), 32.

Questions for Discussion

1. The Exodus was one of the most important episodes in Israelite history. It told how God freed His people from slavery in Egypt and led them through the Red Sea out into the desert where He gave them the Ten Commandments and sealed His covenant with them as His chosen people. The climax comes at the end of the Israelites' forty years of wandering in the desert, when Joshua led the people into the Promised Land which God had prepared for them. Read Joshua 3:14-17.

(a) With this background in mind, what would be the symbolism of John the Baptist's taking people out into the desert and leading them through the Jordan River?

_____

_____

(b) Why might he attract so many people out in this desert area? What hopes might he be stirring in the Jewish people's hearts?

_____

_____

2. Read Malachi 4:5 (some translations, Malachi 3:23). This is the final Old Testament prophecy, and it describes how the prophet Elijah will in some sense return and precede the coming of the Lord. Now read Matthew 3:4 and 2 Kings 1:8. How is John the Baptist described as that new Elijah?

_____

_____

3. Let us now consider how the Old Testament prophets Elijah and Elisha prefigure John the Baptist and Jesus.

(a) According to the following passages, what great things did Elisha do in his ministry?

2 Kings 5:1-19 _____

2 Kings 4:32-38 _____

2 Kings 4:42-44 _____

(b) How would these great works of Elisha prefigure what Jesus did in His ministry?

_____

_____

_____

4. Just as the prophet Elijah preceded the prophet Elisha, who would continue his prophetic ministry and go on to do even greater works, so does John the Baptist prepare the way for Jesus and His new movement, which will begin at the Jordan and quickly surpass John's ministry.

Read 2 Kings 2:6-15. In what ways might this scene prefigure the encounter between Jesus and John at the Jordan?

_____

_____

_____

_____

_____

5. Recall how the word "messiah" means "anointed one," referring to the anointed king of Israel. How might the Spirit's descending on Jesus at His baptism be considered His anointing as the Messiah-King? To help answer this question, read Matthew 3:16-17, 1 Samuel 10:1, 6, and 1 Samuel 16:13. (Isaiah 42:1 and 61:1 also may be helpful.)

_____

_____

_____

6. According to Catechism nos. 1221-23, Christ's baptism was prefigured by Israel's crossing of the Red Sea to escape from Egyptian slavery and their crossing over the Jordan to enter the Promised Land. With this context in mind, how might our own Baptisms be considered an exodus-like event?

_____

_____

_____

7. Catechism, no. 1241 describes how we are incorporated into Christ's kingly mission at our Baptism. What do you think this means? What are our responsibilities as baptized Christians?

_____

_____

_____

_____

3

Battle in the Desert
—Matthew 4—

In Matthew 4, we see that Jesus began His career with a very bold opening move.

Notice how Jesus did not start His public ministry by teaching in the synagogue or preaching in the streets. Nor did He begin by performing miraculous works such as healing the sick, walking on the water, or raising the dead. Rather, the very first thing Jesus chose to do was to confront the devil. And this is quite significant.

After His baptism in the Jordan River, Jesus traveled out into the desert to fast and pray for forty days, and there He was tempted three times by Satan. What was the significance of this cryptic dual between the King of Kings and the prince of this world? In this famous scene, we will see how Jesus fights His first battle as the Messiah-King, but He does so in a way that may have caught many first-century Jews by surprise.

The Lion King

In Matthew 3, Jesus' baptism marked the beginning of His messianic mission. There at the Jordan, the Spirit descended upon Him, just as the Spirit descended on Israel's monarchs when they were anointed as kings. As we saw in the last chapter, Jesus was thus identified as the "Anointed One" or "Messiah." But what were the Jews expecting the Messiah-King to do? Since Israel's kings were often associated with fighting Israel's battles, the Jews thought that the sending of a Messiah-King would be part of God's plan to restore Israel and free them from the pagan nations.

This, after all, is what the great Israelite kings of old had done. For example, King David defeated Goliath and the Philistines. King Hezekiah kept the Assyrian armies at bay. King Josiah lost his life in a battle against the Egyptians. Judas Maccabeus established his dynasty by leading a guerrilla war-like campaign against the Syrians, driving their pagan idolatry out of the Temple and out of Jerusalem. As one can see, the great kings of Israel were known for protecting God's people from the oppression of their pagan neighbors.

Looking to the future, the Psalms and the prophets foretold how God would send another great king to do the same. This heir would establish his dominion by triumphing over the pagan nations. From the fall of the Davidic monarchy to the time of Jesus, these scriptural texts fueled Jewish hopes for a renewed Davidic dynasty. God would send a new king who would free the Israelites from their enemies, reestablish Israel in the Promised Land, and bring blessing to the world (Ps. 2:8; 72:8-11, 17; 110:6; Is. 9:1-7; 11:1-10; Ezek. 34; Dan. 9).

A Holy War?

This certainly was good news for Jews in Jesus' day. After centuries of foreign domination, they longed for the renewal of the Davidic dynasty and anxiously anticipated the coming of the great king who would liberate Israel.

Some Jews in the century before Jesus even put their hopes down on paper, writing texts of their own which described how God would send a king who would lead them into triumph over their enemies. They told stories about how this king would smash the Gentiles like one would smash a potter's jar into pieces. The Messiah would come out of the forest like a lion to deliver the faithful Jews from the hands of the Romans. Indeed, this "holy war" theology surrounded many Jewish longings for the restoration of Israel.

But was this the type of liberation Jesus would offer?

A Surprise Attack

Like the great kings who went before Him, Jesus as the Messiah-King did enter into a battle of His own. But the type of battle Jesus came to fight was very different from what many of His contemporaries were expecting. Instead of confronting the Romans—who were the evil oppressors of the Jews in Jesus' day Jesus marched into the desert to combat a much fiercer opponent: *the devil.*

The account in Matthew 4 of Jesus' overcoming the three temptations of the devil would remind the careful reader that the real enemy of Israel was much bigger than the Roman Empire or any other pagan nation. The true enemy was the power of sin and Satan. This might have come as a surprise to a number of Jewish leaders who focused on resisting Rome and were anticipating a Messiah who would lead them in battle against their pagan oppressors.

However, by beginning His public ministry with a showdown with the devil, Jesus shows us what type of Messiah-King He will be. It is true that He was coming to start a revolution, but it was not a militaristic one. His revolution was internal, inside the hearts and minds of God's people, freeing them from the bondage of sin.

Here, Jesus is simply acting in accordance with what the Jewish law and prophets said about Israel's situation in the first century. Israel's suffering under foreign occupation was actually a symptom of a much deeper illness. Unfaithfulness to God brought on the exile and the fall of the Davidic monarchy. To focus on driving out the Romans would be to miss the point. Violent revolution would not solve the problem. As one New Testament scholar explains, "to drive out paganism with paganism's weapons is already to lose the battle."[1]

Thus Jesus came not to fight the Romans, but to treat the root of the problem: the sin of Israel and the sin of all humanity. If sin were conquered, Israel truly would be free. This explains why Jesus set out into the desert to lock heads with the personification of all evil, the devil himself.

Desert Storm

As the Messiah-King, Jesus would have been viewed by His Jewish followers as their representative. Throughout Israel's history, the king was considered an embodiment of the whole nation. So closely was the king associated with his people that what happened to the king could be said to have happened to

---

[1] N.T. Wright, *Jesus: The New Way* (Worcester, MA: Christian History Institute, 1998), 52.

the people as a whole. For example, when the king was faithful to the covenant with Yahweh, the entire nation received God's blessings. But when the king sinned greatly, the whole nation suffered for his infidelity. The king represented the people. This helps us to understand Jesus' temptations in the desert. As Israel's royal representative, Jesus experienced the same trials Israel did during the Exodus. What happened to Israel in the time of Moses happened to Jesus in the first century.

The fact that Jesus spent forty days in the desert shows how He symbolically relived the story of Israel's forty years in the wilderness during the Exodus. Furthermore, upon closer examination of Jesus' three temptations, we will see that Jesus faced the same trials Israel faced in the desert, entering into the drama of Israel's weaknesses and failings during their pilgrimage to the Promised Land (cf. Catechism, no. 538).[2]

But then Jesus gave that story a surprise ending. Instead of stumbling like the ancient people of God did, He proved Himself to be a faithful Israelite. Jesus remained faithful precisely where Israel had been unfaithful. As such, Jesus symbolically unties the knot of Israel's sin. In His battle with Satan in these three temptations, Jesus "pre-enacts" what He ultimately will do for Israel on the Cross: conquer sin and defeat the devil. This is the real battle Jesus fights and the real liberation which He offers.

---

[2] See also Jack Dean Kingsbury, *Matthew as Story* (Philadelphia: Fortress Press, 1988), 55.

Three Strikes, He's Out

Let's take a closer look at how the three temptations of Jesus relate to the first three major trials of
Israel in the Exodus. Here we will see that the failings
of Israel are symbolically overcome by Jesus' victory
over the devil.

(1) *Israel's first test.* The first of Israel's trials
involved hunger. After Moses parted the Red Sea and
led the Israelites out of Egypt and into the desert, the
people celebrated their newfound freedom.
However, they soon faced another problem: How
would they find food in this desert? Their rejoicing
quickly turned into panic. Instead of trusting in God
to provide, the people turned against Moses, saying
"[Y]ou have brought us out into this wilderness to kill
this whole assembly with hunger" (Ex. 16:3).

Jesus' first test. Similarly, Jesus faced hunger in
His first temptation as the devil tried to get Him to
use His power as the Son of God to break His forty
days of fasting. The Father sent the Spirit to lead
Jesus into the desert to pray and fast for forty days.
For Jesus to turn the stones into bread would be to
exercise His messianic authority for His own self-
interest and thus depart from the Father's will.
Unlike Israel, who doubted that God would provide
for their needs in the wilderness, Jesus does not
waver from trusting the Father. He quotes
Deuteronomy 8:3 (a passage that brings to mind the
story of Israel's first test), saying "Man shall not live
by bread alone" (Mt. 4:4). As the people's royal representative, Jesus overcomes the first major fall of
Israel in the desert.

Passing the Test

(2) *Israel's second test.* The second trial involved Israel putting God "to the test." After God provided for Israel's nourishment by sending them bread from heaven (manna), the people soon faced another dilemma: How were they going to find water to drink in the dry desert? Once again, instead of putting their trust in Yahweh to provide for their needs, they doubted Him and accused Moses of orchestrating a vicious plot against them: "Why did you bring us up out of Egypt, to kill us and our children and our cattle with thirst?" (Ex. 17:3). God responded by giving them water from a rock, and He named the place of this second ordeal "Massah," which means "testing." There, the people unjustly tested God's trustworthiness, which is absolute and would not be questioned by the truly faithful Israelite.

Jesus' second test. This corresponds to Jesus' second temptation when the devil challenged Him to throw Himself down from the pinnacle of the Temple to see if God's angels would really save Him. Satan said to Jesus, "If you are the Son of God, throw yourself down; for it is written, 'He will give his angels charge of you'" (Mt. 4:6). Unlike the Israelites at Massah, Jesus refused to test God on this or any other issue. Jesus had absolute confidence in the Father and had no desire to test Him. This is why He viewed this second temptation as parallel to Israel's second trial in the desert. He responds to the devil by quoting part of Deuteronomy 6:16. When we consider this verse as a whole, we see that Jesus had Israel's second testing at Massah in mind: "You shall not put the Lord your God to the test, *as you tested him at Massah*" (Deut. 6:16).

As such, Jesus overcomes Israel's second failing by refusing to test God in this second temptation.

(3) *Israel's third test.* The last temptation of Israel involved worshipping a false god. This came in the golden calf episode at Mount Sinai. After Moses left the people for forty days to go up the mountain and receive the Ten Commandments, the people down below did not know what happened to their leader and feared he had died. Failing to trust Yahweh again, they built an idol in the shape of a golden calf, putting their trust in an Egyptian pagan deity.

Jesus' third test. Similarly, in the third test, Satan tempted Jesus to worship him in exchange for all the kingdoms of the world. Jesus refused to worship a false god and responded by alluding to Deuteronomy 6:13-14, saying "You shall worship the Lord your God and him only shall you serve" (Mt. 4:10). In this third temptation, Jesus overcomes Israel's sin of idolatry.

The Victory of Jesus

As the first act of His messiahship, Jesus' victory over the devil sets the tone for the rest of His public ministry. Most of Jesus' subsequent actions— whether His healings, His forgiving people's sins, or His exorcisms—can be seen as repercussions of His initial triumph over the devil in the desert. Jesus will go from town to town carrying out His victory over the devil in the lives of the people He meets. In touching the lives of the sick, the crippled, the blind, or the great sinners and demoniacs, Jesus frees them from the power and effects of sin, so that they may experience God's victory in their own lives. All this, of course, points to Jesus' work on the Cross, where He definitively conquers the prince of this world and wins salvation for all humanity (cf. Jn. 12:31).

The Church's annual celebration of Lent helps us experience the victory of Jesus in our own lives today. Each year, in the forty days of Lent, Christians participate in Jesus' forty days of prayer, fasting, and trial in the desert. Through our prayer and mortification, we too prepare to battle sin. But the question we must ask ourselves—in Lent or any other time of the year—is whether we will be like Israel in the desert, failing to put our trust in God, or like Jesus, faithful to Our Heavenly Father, so that we may experience the abundant blessings of the victory Christ won for us on Easter Sunday.

✝ ✝ ✝

Questions for Discussion

1. According to the following passages, what did the Jews believe the promised Davidic king would do?

Psalm 2:1-9 _____

Psalm 72:8-11, 17_____

Psalm 110:5-6 _____

2. According to some Jews in the first century, who would be the enemies that the Messiah-King would conquer?

_____

_____

_____

_____

3. In Matthew 4, Jesus goes out to fight Israel's most important battle. But whom does Jesus show to be the real enemy of God's people?

_____

_____

_____

4. Keeping in mind that Israel's kings were viewed as representing or personifying the people as a whole, let's examine how Jesus as the Messiah-King symbolically reverses Israel's sins in the desert from the time of Moses.

(a) Read Exodus 16:1-3. How does Jesus symbolically overcome this sin of Israel in the first temptation He faces in the desert in Matthew 4:1-4?

_____

_____

_____

_____

(b) Read Exodus 17:1-7. Recall that the location where this event took place is known as "Massah," which literally means "testing," since this is where the Israelites tested the Lord (Ex. 17:2, 7). How might this scene be in the background of Jesus' second temptation in Matthew 4:5-7?

_____

_____

_____

(c) Read Exodus 32:1-4. How might Matthew 4:8-10 show Jesus overturning Israel's sin of idolatry at Mount Sinai by resisting this third temptation of the devil?

_____

_____

_____

5. We saw how Israel did not trust in God to provide for their needs, and thus they fell three times in the desert. But Jesus' full confidence in the Father allowed Him to resist the temptations of the devil.

(a) What are some areas in our own lives where we might lack confidence in God? Where is it difficult to let go and trust in God to provide for us?

_____

_____

_____

_____

(b) Why is it sometimes difficult to trust in God?

_____

_____

_____

(c) Read Matthew 6:25-33. What do these verses tell us about God's fatherly care for us?

_____

_____

(d) In light of these verses, how can we be more like Jesus, confidently placing our lives in the Father's hands?

_____

_____

_____

_____

4

THE CHALLENGE OF THE KINGDOM
—MATTHEW 5-7—

The famous "Sermon on the Mount" (Mt. 5-7) is best known for its beautiful spiritual and moral teachings. Indeed, it would be hard to beat a sermon that had the Beatitudes, the Our Father, and the command to love your enemy all packed into one!

One thing, however, which is not commonly noted about the Sermon on the Mount is how explosive its message was and how Jesus' words would have shaken the world of many who were listening to Him on the Galilean hillside that day.

A New Vision

"Love your enemy." "Blessed are the merciful." "Turn the other cheek." With these words, Jesus was not simply setting forth a brand new, lofty ethical standard. While Christ's teachings in the Sermon on the Mount certainly have great moral applications for Christians of all ages, we must see how Jesus was giving a very specific challenge to the people of His day. Jesus was offering a new vision—a new vision for what it meant to be God's people.

National Crisis

The Jews in Jesus' day were living in hard times. They were facing a national crisis. Roman rulers controlled their land, took their money, and raped their women. Many of the Jewish priests and local leaders were assassinated and replaced by handpicked appointments from Rome or Herod. Thousands of

Jews who tried to resist Roman rule quickly paid the severe price of death.

This oppressive environment created numerous challenges for those who were striving to remain loyal to God's covenant. According to the Torah, God alone was king and He would rule His people through a descendant of King David. No foreigner was to rule over the Jews (Deut. 17:15). So what was a good Jew to do? Was it okay to go along with the Roman authorities, or would submitting to Caesar, Pilate, and Herod betray Yahweh's lordship?

Then came the question of taxes and tithes. With the Romans imposing heavy tax burdens, it would be quite difficult for many Jews to pay both the taxes to Caesar and the tithe, which their own law required them to give to God. So should one be faithful to Rome or to Yahweh?

Also, there was the risk of assimilation. When the Romans imported thousands of their own citizens, with their pagan practices and lifestyles, right into the midst of Jewish society, it became increasingly difficult for Jews to maintain their identity as God's holy people set apart from the nations. Any time a smaller culture is enveloped by a larger, dominating culture, assimilation is a real danger. Thus, Jewish self-preservation was a critical issue in the time of Jesus.

Diverse Strategies

The Jewish people responded to this crisis in different ways. While they all believed that one day God would rescue those who remained faithful to the covenant, there were diverse opinions about who those faithful Jews would be. One burning question in first-century Judaism was: "What does it mean to be a true, loyal Jew during this time of oppression?" One group, the Pharisees, said faithfulness meant imitating God's holiness. In Hebrew, "holy" literally means "set apart" or "separated," and the Pharisees imitated God's holiness by separating themselves from anything or anyone that was unholy. They did this through strict observance of the laws in a way that would clearly distinguish the Jews from their pagan neighbors. Thus, they avoided certain types of foods, certain types of animals, certain types of utensils and, most of all, certain types of people, such as sinners, tax collectors, and Gentiles (non-Jews). Little details such as these—what you ate, how you ate it, and with whom you ate—were all-powerful political and religious symbols. These were symbolic ways of expressing faithfulness to God's covenant in the midst of a growing pagan culture. They were ways of saying, "I am not like the pagans. I am a true Jew, part of God's faithful people."

The Essenes were another group who emphasized separateness—but to an even greater degree. They called for separation from society altogether. With Roman occupation and corrupt Jewish leaders in Jerusalem, remaining holy within society was no longer a possibility. Many Essenes withdrew to the desert, where they established a monastic-like community, claiming to be the only Israelites left who were still faithful to God's covenant.

Other Jews believed holiness could be obtained only by driving the Romans out of the land. These revolutionaries stressed that only Yahweh was meant to be king over Israel. To submit to Caesar or Herod would be to reject God's role as Israel's true king. Thus, many Jews were ready to take up arms against the Romans when the time was right.

Setting the Stage

One can see there was much diversity in first-century Judaism. Although most people believed that God would rescue the loyal Jews during the time of the Messiah, there were various opinions about what it meant to be part of that faithful remnant when the kingdom finally arrived. This was the complex stage onto which Jesus entered when He began His kingdom movement in a northern region of Israel called Galilee, preaching "Repent, for the kingdom of heaven is at hand" (Mt. 4:17).

Go Tell It on a Mountain

From the beginning, Jesus' public ministry took off like lightning. People from all over Galilee and beyond flocked to see Him. Why was He so popular? His message and His actions said it all: The long-awaited kingdom was now arriving (Mt. 4:17, 23-25). Jesus was offering a message the Jews were longing to hear. With eager anticipation, many Jews began to place their hopes in Him to rescue them from their enemies and restore the kingdom to Israel. No wonder Jesus' fame spread throughout the region so rapidly!

After attracting this large following, Jesus decided to lead the crowds up a mountain in Galilee for a special discourse about the kingdom. This action itself could have led some of His followers to ponder what might happen next. In those days, the hill country of Galilee was a refuge for Jewish revolutionaries who were plotting their assaults against foreign oppressors. The caves in those hills made for good hiding places. Not too long before this, a group of bandits had hidden in the Galilean hills during a fierce conflict with King Herod.

So when Jesus led His followers up a mountain in Galilee, perhaps a few may have been wondering whether He was going to start some type of revolt of His own—like Judas the Galilean had done in the Galilean hillside one generation earlier. Was Jesus going to make a claim to be Israel's king and lead the people in a fight for the kingdom? The crowd waited for Him to speak.

The Kingdom Movement

Jesus then began to address His band of followers on the mountainside with a startling message. He introduced an unexpected lineup of people who would be blessed in the kingdom He was building: "Blessed are the merciful . . . Blessed are the peace makers . . . Blessed are those who are persecuted" (Mt. 5:7, 9-10).

What a shock. What kind of kingdom movement was this? Jesus seemed to be blessing all the wrong people. The peacemakers, the merciful, and the persecuted were not the expected first-round draft choices for a kingdom-building team. Many would have preferred vengeance over mercy, vindication over persecution, and fighting for freedom over making peace.

Consider a few other famous commands in the Sermon on the Mount, such as "love your enemy," "pray for those who persecute you," and the so-called "go the extra mile" (Mt. 5:41, 44). Sometimes these teachings are misunderstood as practical instructions for becoming pushovers for Jesus. But in their first-century context, these challenges would have been much more intense. In these commands, Jesus was subverting the revolutionary and nationalistic tendencies which pervaded much of first-century Judaism.

The Challenge

For example, "love your enemy" (cf. Mt. 5:44) was not simply an abstract principle to be applied when you had to face someone who wanted to do you harm. Rather this command had a specific, concrete meaning for the Jews who heard His teaching that day. For those original listeners, "love your enemy" would have sounded something like: "Love the Romans who persecute you. Love Herod and His illegitimate, violent monarchy. Do not join the revolt movements."

Similarly, the command "[I]f any one forces you to go one mile, go with him two miles" (Mt. 5:41) was not simply a lesson on being generous. Roman soldiers often forced civilians to carry their gear for one mile. Using this image, Jesus challenged the Jews to go above and beyond the call of duty and generously serve even their cruel Roman oppressors. He was exhorting them not to view their foreign enemies as adversaries to be overcome, but as brothers and sisters who are to be loved and won over for God.

In fact, that was Israel's mission from the very beginning: to be light to the world and salt of the earth (Mt. 5:13-14; Is. 42:6, 49:6). Jesus challenged the people to return to their roots and to be what Israel was always meant to be—not an exclusive, nationalistic religion isolated from the other nations, but a priestly kingdom serving the Gentiles and leading them to worship the one true God (cf. Ex. 19:5-6).

Light of the World

Israel was meant to be light to the world, God's instrument to bless the nations. But in the time of Jesus, many had lost sight of Israel's worldwide mission. Israel's light had turned inward on itself, focusing more on remaining ritually pure and separated from the pagans—as in the Pharisaic and Essene program— or intent on driving out the Romans with force, as in the resistance movement. How could Israel be light to the world if they were more concerned about fighting off the world?

Jesus shattered the prevailing views of the day with this challenge:

> You are the light of the world. A city set on a hill cannot be hid. Nor do men light a lamp and put it under a bushel, but on a stand, and it gives light to all in the house. Let your light so shine before men (Mt. 5:14-16).

The way of the kingdom was the way of peace, and it involved gathering together all peoples, even the Jewish oppressors. Rome and Herod were not enemies to be conquered, but brethren to be gathered back into God's covenant family.

The Two Ways

This can be seen more clearly when we consider how Matthew's Gospel presents Jesus as a new Moses. Both Jesus and Moses escaped an evil ruler's decree to kill Israelite children by going to the Egyptians. Both came out of Egypt to return to Israel. Both went out into the desert, Moses for forty years and Jesus for forty days. More Mosaic parallels are found in Jesus' first and last discourses: the Sermon on the Mount (Mt. 5-7) and His confrontation with the Pharisees in the Temple (Mt. 23).

Consider this: Before his death, Moses gave the people of Israel the covenant of Deuteronomy just when they were getting ready to enter the Promised Land after forty years in the wilderness. In his parting words, Moses left Israel with a choice: faithfulness or unfaithfulness to the covenant, life or death, blessing or curse:

> I have set before you life and death, blessing and curse; therefore choose life, that you and your descendants may live, loving the LORD your God, obeying his voice, and cleaving to him (Deut. 30:19-20).

Moses gave instructions for this covenant to be announced and ratified on two mountains after the people entered the land. Half the tribes of Israel shouted out the covenant blessings on Mount Ebal, while the other half proclaimed the curses on Mount Gerizim (Deut. 27:11-13). Israel had to choose which path she would follow. Faithfulness would bring blessing upon Israel in their land. Unfaithfulness would invite the curses and expulsion from the land. They ended up choosing the latter, and Jews in the time of Jesus believed they were still suffering the consequences of their sin in their experience of foreign oppression.

In similar fashion, Jesus announced blessings and curses from two different mountains of His own. He offered seven blessings in the beatitudes on the Galilean mountain at the beginning of His ministry (Mt. 5:3-12).[1] And He announced seven curses on the Temple Mount in Jerusalem near the end of His ministry. There, Jesus pronounced the seven "woes" on those scribes and Pharisees who rejected His kingdom program (Mt. 23:13-36).[2]

The message is clear. Once again, Israel was faced with a vital decision. Like Moses, Jesus forced the Jews of His day to make a choice: "Do you want to follow the way of the revolutionaries and separatists? Or will you follow My way—the way of mercy, peace, and enduring persecution?" The first way will lead to Israel's destruction. The latter will lead to the kingdom's restoration. Ultimately for Jesus, as we will see, the road to the kingdom is the way of the Cross.

* * *

---

[1] The eighth beatitude has the same blessing as the first ("the kingdom of heaven"), giving a total of seven blessings in the beatitudes.
[2] Peter Ellis, *Matthew: His Mind and His Message* (Collegeville, MN: Liturgical Press, 1974), 81.

Questions for Discussion

1. In what sense were the Jews facing a national crisis in the first century? What problems did the Jewish people face by living under Roman occupation with Caesar ruling as king over them, with the empire demanding heavy taxes from the people and with many Gentiles polluting their culture by bringing their pagan practices right into God's holy land?

_____

_____

_____

2. Based on this chapter's reflections, how did some groups within first-century Judaism respond to the crisis? Consider the following groups:

(a) Pharisees _____

(b) Essenes _____

(c) Revolutionaries _____

3. If you were a Jew in the time of Jesus, how would you have responded to this national crisis? Would you have followed the way of the Pharisees? The Essenes? The revolutionaries?

_____

_____

_____

4. How open do you think you might have been to Jesus' message and the type of kingdom He was initiating?

_____

_____

5. Read Matthew 4:23-25. These verses serve as an overture for the next five chapters of Matthew's Gospel, summarizing the major themes in Jesus' growing movement in Galilee. According to this passage, how did Jesus go about announcing His kingdom?

_____

_____

_____

_____

6. Read the Beatitudes in Matthew 5:3-12. How would these verses have been understood in their first-century Jewish context? Why would these blessings have been somewhat shocking to some Jews?

_____

_____

_____

7. What was at the heart of Jesus' challenge for Israel in the Sermon on the Mount?

_____

_____

_____

8. How do Jesus' commands to love your enemy, forgive those who persecute you, and "go the extra mile" fit into this challenge?

_____

_____

_____

9. Read Jesus' challenge to Israel in Matthew 5:14-16.

(a) Saint Paul describes the Church as the new "Israel of God" (Gal. 6:16). In what ways is the Catholic Church called to live out Christ's challenge and be the "light of the world"?

_____

_____

_____

(b) What specifically can _we_ do to let our light shine before all?

_____

_____

_____

5

PUTTING THE KINGDOM INTO ACTION
—MATTHEW 8-9—

It has often been said that "actions speak louder than words." This maxim is especially true for Jesus in the whirlwind of events following the famous "Sermon on the Mount."

In this great sermon, Jesus challenged Israel to be "light to the world" and confronted the exclusive and nationalistic tendencies within the Judaism of His day. However, while His words certainly left a deep impression on many, they were only a prelude to the more dramatic actions which followed when Jesus came down from that mountain. Matthew 8-9 records for us how Jesus immediately put His words into action. He performed ten miracles which shouted out a message that was much louder than anything He said in His sermon. In remarkable fashion, Jesus cured a leper, healed a paralytic, restored sight to the blind, raised a child from the dead, and expelled demons. At the end of this *tour de force*, the crowds marveled, saying "Never was anything like this seen in Israel" (Mt. 9:33).

What was Jesus saying in these mighty deeds? Was Jesus trying to establish Himself as some type of first-century faith healer? Did He perform these miracles simply to impress people or perhaps to prove His divinity? Looking at these powerful actions through the lenses of first-century Judaism, we will see how practically every move Jesus made was charged with great symbolic meaning and played a key part in His plan of building His kingdom.

John the Baptist's Question

John the Baptist had the same questions we do. He was wondering about the meaning behind Jesus' mighty works. John heard about these miracles while he was in prison for having preached against the wicked deeds of King Herod. In this time of persecution and suffering, John's faith was tested, and he had some uncertainties about whether Jesus really was the Messiah. John might have been wondering, "If Jesus really is the Messiah-King, why am I still suffering here in prison? Why hasn't He freed me from Herod's terror?"

Wanting some reassurance from Jesus, John sent some of his own disciples to ask Jesus, "Are you he who is to come, or shall we look for another?" (Mt. 11:3). Jesus gave this answer to them:

> Go and tell John what you hear and see: the blind receive their sight and the lame walk, lepers are cleansed and the deaf hear, and the dead are raised up, and the poor have good news preached to them (Mt. 11:4-5).

What kind of response was that? How would these words have answered John's important question? At first glance, Jesus does not seem to be very helpful. Yet those who know the Old Testament—and John the Baptist certainly did!—would realize that Jesus was echoing a prophecy from Isaiah concerning the restoration of Israel:

> Behold, your God will come. . . . He will come and save you. Then the eyes of the blind shall be opened, and the ears of the deaf unstopped; then

shall the lame man leap like a hart, and the tongue of the dumb sing for joy (Is. 35:4-6).

Jesus basically said to the disciples, "Go tell John what you have seen and heard—in other words, tell him that Isaiah 35 has come to fulfillment in Me." That certainly would have provided the reassurance John was seeking. And this provides us with an insight into how Jesus interpreted His own actions: They were signs of Israel's restoration. In these healings, Jesus was symbolically announcing the arrival of the long-awaited kingdom.

Don't Make Essenc!
What is also significant is the type of people Jesus healed. Jews who suffered from leprosy and other illnesses would have been the outcasts in Jesus' day. They were excluded from society because they were ritually unclean. Only the pure and the physically whole were considered full Israelites.

This attitude was reflected in the writings of one Jewish sect known as the Essenes. Consider the following fragment from a group of ancient Essene manuscripts (commonly called the Dead Sea Scrolls), which lists the type of people who were excluded from office in their community:

No man smitten in his flesh,
or paralysed in his feet or hands,
or lame, or blind,
or deaf, or dumb,
or smitten in his flesh with a visible blemish . . .

none of these shall come to hold office among the
congregation.[1]

In this light, we see that Jesus' healing ministry
went far beyond curing bodily ailments. Jesus was
bringing these outsiders in. By healing them physically, He was restoring them socially and religiously
back into Israelite society. In this way, Jesus was
symbolically showing how all the traditional outcasts
were among the first to be included in His kingdom.

Reach Out and Touch Someone

Let's look at the leper who knelt down before Jesus
and begged Him to make him clean (Mt. 8:1-4).
Leprosy was the most dreaded disease in ancient
Judaism. Lepers were banished from society. They
were considered untouchables who had to announce
that they were approaching by shouting out, "Unclean,
unclean!" If a Jew touched a leper, he himself would
become ritually unclean and would have to go
through a complex process of ritual purification
before being fit for Temple worship again.

Yet when this particular leper asked Jesus to heal
him, Jesus did the unthinkable. He stretched out His
hand and touched the man! But then, something
amazing happened. Instead of becoming ritually
defiled Himself, Jesus' holiness overpowered the
uncleanness of the leper and the leper was cured. It
was not Jesus who was made unclean by touching the
leper, but the leper was made clean by touching Jesus!

---

[1] 1QSa2.5-9 in Geza Vermes, *The Complete Dead Sea Scrolls in English*
(New York: Allen Lange The Penguin Press, 1997), 159.

In another episode, a woman suffering from a hemorrhage for twelve years desperately approached Jesus for healing. But she had to do so in a secretive way. With this ailment, the woman daily faced not only the physical danger of blood loss, but also the cultural shame of ritual uncleanness (cf. Lev. 15:25-30). She knew that any contact with Jesus would make Him ritually unclean as well. Nevertheless, she said to herself, "If I only touch his garment, I shall be made well" and dared to come up from behind and touch the fringe of His garment in the hope of being cured (Mt. 9:21).

First-century Jews would have been shocked by such a daring action. They would have assumed that Jesus became defiled by coming into contact with her uncleanness. Once again, however, the opposite occurred. Instead of Jesus' becoming contaminated by her ritual impurity, the woman was healed instantly by the power of Jesus. Jesus had a healing power that far exceeded anything ever seen in the Old Testament. His holiness transformed the unholy. His cleanness wiped out the uncleanness. His sinlessness even purified sin.[2]

Forgiving Sins

As His fame spread throughout the region of Galilee, crowds flocked to Jesus and begged Him for help. The sick asked Jesus for cures. Blind men cried out to Him for sight. Gentile officials asked Him to heal their children.

---

[2] Marcus Borg, *The Politics of Holiness* (Harrisburg: Trinity Press, 1988), 148.

At the same time, Matthew tells the story of a paralyzed man who could not draw near to Jesus. His generous friends, however, carried him to Jesus for help. Jesus, in turn, gave the man something much greater than anything he probably ever imagined. Not only did Jesus cure the man of his physical disability and give him the strength to stand up and walk, but Jesus also bestowed on him the power to walk again spiritually by forgiving his sins:

> And behold, they brought to him a paralytic, lying on his bed; and when Jesus saw their faith he said to the paralytic, "Take heart, my son; your sins are forgiven" (Mt. 9:2).

By forgiving this man's sins, Jesus deliberately engaged in an action that was extremely provocative. It shouted out good news, but in a way that might have alarmed some of those who witnessed this amazing event.

Forgiveness of sins surely was one of the chief signs of the New Covenant. Recall how the Jews interpreted their suffering under foreign domination as resulting from their own sinfulness (cf. Deut. 28:15-68; Dan. 9:1-19). That's why several prophecies from the Old Testament spoke of a New Covenant in which God would free Israel from their oppression and do so by freeing Israel from their sins (cf. Jer. 31:31-34; 33:4-11; Ezek. 36:25-27; Dan. 9:24). Forgiveness of sins and Israel's restoration went hand in hand. So when Jesus forgave sins, He was not simply bestowing private spiritual blessings on privileged individuals. Rather, He was announcing the fulfillment of everything the Jews were hoping for. By offering forgiveness of sins,

Jesus was symbolically announcing the dawn of the New Covenant and the arrival of the long-awaited kingdom. Indeed, this was good news!

Replacing the Temple

But not everyone took it that way. Instead of rejoicing, the scribes accused Jesus of blasphemy (Mt. 9:3). They believed that only God could forgive sins and He did so through the Temple priests and the Temple sacrifices. "Who does this man think He is, forgiving sins apart from the Temple?" they would ask.

Thus, in this simple action of saying "your sins are forgiven," Jesus claimed to do only what God could do. And He was saying to the Jews, "What you used to get at the Temple in Jerusalem and through the levitical priesthood you can get right here, right now, with Me." In one broad stroke, Jesus bypassed the Temple system altogether and proclaimed Himself the source of forgiveness of sins. Jesus made Himself the new Temple, hinting that the days of the Temple in Jerusalem might be coming to an end. No wonder the scribes were so upset!

An Open Table

In addition to healing the sick and forgiving the sins of the people, Jesus was busy building His kingdom even while eating at the dinner table. Throughout His ministry, Jesus invited sinners and other outcasts of society to share a meal with Him. This practice of open table fellowship, however, was much more than a gesture of warm hospitality. It was a revolutionary action which sparked much controversy. Consider this scene in Matthew 9:

And as he sat at table in the house, behold, many tax
collectors and sinners came and sat down with Jesus
and his disciples. And when the Pharisees saw this,
they said to his disciples, "Why does your teacher
eat with tax collectors and sinners?" (Mt. 9:10-11).

Why were the Pharisees so upset? To understand
their perspective, we need to know a little about the
sacredness of meals in the first century.

More Than a Mouthful

We can't overestimate the importance of eating
with "the right people" in first-century Judaism. In
ancient Israel, meals were sacred. To invite someone to a meal was practically to invite them into
your family.

In our modern society, we can sit down in a fast-
food restaurant and have a meal alongside complete
strangers and not think much about it. However, the
ancient Israelites considered eating a meal with others a rather serious affair. Shared food and drink
symbolized a shared life. They forged covenant
bonds and were interpreted as establishing familial
relationships—so much so that two enemies could
seal a peace agreement by sharing a meal and then,
afterwards, even refer to each other as brothers! (cf.
Gen. 26:26-31; 31:54-55). That's why the Jews generally ate only with extended family members or
fellow Israelites of a similar social and religious class.
Most loyal Jews never ate with pagans or sinners.

More than any other group, the Pharisees gave special attention to table fellowship laws. In their desire
to remain separate from anything or anyone unholy,

the Pharisees taught that Jews should only eat with fellow Jews who were in good standing. In fact, 229 of their 341 laws dealt with table fellowship alone!

This helps explain why the Pharisees were so scandalized when Jesus ate with the sinners and tax collectors. How could Jesus sit at table with grave sinners who were ritually unclean and outside the covenant? How could Jesus share a meal with the tax collectors, who were known as the traitors who collaborated with Rome and Herod and took the Jewish people's money for the enemy?

So when Jesus dined at table, He seemed to be celebrating His kingdom with all the wrong people. A true Jew would never think of doing such a thing!

The Doctor's Orders

However, in these eloquent actions, Jesus was making a bold statement. He deliberately chose these controversial dining partners to highlight the universality of His mission and to demonstrate His power to transform sinners and welcome them back into covenant fellowship.

Notice how Jesus responded to the Pharisees' complaint: "It is not the healthy who need the doctor, but the sick" (Mt. 9:12).[3] Just as a doctor must have contact with the sick, so does Jesus draw near to sinners to restore them to spiritual health. In this sense, His practice of eating with sinners and tax collectors signified a greater miracle than His healing of blindness, leprosy, and other illnesses. Without saying a word,

---

[3] This quote was taken from the *New Jerusalem Bible*.

Jesus symbolically restored these outcasts to God's covenant family and announced a surprise cast of members in the kingdom He was building.

Once again, His actions spoke louder than His words.

* * *

Questions for Discussion

1. Some readers of the Gospel miss the central points of Jesus' mission because they focus primarily on His teachings and not on His actions. Israel's great prophets, however, often communicated their message not only in words, but also in symbolic actions. Consider the following examples of prophetic symbolic action in the Old Testament:

(a) Jeremiah 19:1-5, 10-13. What is the symbolism of Jeremiah's action in this passage?

_____

_____

(b) Ezekiel 12:1-13. What is the symbolism of Ezekiel's action?

_____

_____

2. Why would this idea of prophetic symbolic actions be important for understanding Jesus' work in Matthew 8-9?

_____

_____

3. Jesus' healings were also symbolic.

(a) Read Isaiah 35:4-6. According to Isaiah, what will be the signs that God is coming to save His people?

_____

_____

_____

_____

(b) Read Matthew 11:2-6. With the prophecy from Isaiah 35 in mind, how does Jesus' response answer John the Baptist's question? What is Jesus symbolically saying in His healing ministry?

_____

_____

_____

4. Read Matthew 9:1-8.

(a) Why were the scribes so upset when Jesus forgave this paralyzed man's sins? By offering forgiveness of sins apart from the entire Temple system, what was Jesus saying about the Temple, its priesthood, and the sacrifices?

_____

_____

_____

(b) Read Jeremiah 31:31-34. In this passage, forgiveness of sins was a chief sign of the New Covenant God promised to bring about. With this background in mind, what would be the symbolism of Jesus' forgiving sins? How would forgiving the sins of this

individual man stir up great hopes for the people of
Israel as a whole?

_____

_____

_____

5. Read Matthew 9:18-22.

(a) In light of the ritual purity laws in Leviticus
15:25-27, what would most Jews think about the
hemorrhaging woman touching Jesus' garment?

_____

_____

_____

(b) What would they think happened to Jesus when
she touched Him?

_____

_____

_____

(c) In light of the reflections in this chapter, what
does Jesus' healing her illness symbolize?

_____

_____

_____

6. Saint Francis of Assisi told his followers to
preach the Gospel always, and when necessary use
words. What do you think this means? What do you
think is the proper balance between words and
actions in sharing the Gospel in today's world? How

might the way Jesus used words in the Sermon on the Mount in Matthew 5-7 and powerful deeds in Matthew 8-9 shed light on this question?

_____

_____

_____

_____

7. Read Matthew 9:10-12. As we have seen, many pious Jews did not want to associate with non-Jews and other grave sinners.

(a) In what ways might faithful Christians today be tempted to fall into a similar trap?

_____

_____

_____

_____

(b) While the Gospels never describe Jesus as associating with sinners in the midst of their sinful actions, they do tell of Jesus constantly welcoming them and warmly inviting them into His table fellowship. How might Jesus' outreach to sinners serve as a model for the Christian's relationship with unbelievers and those who may not be living out their Christian life?

_____

_____

_____

_____

(c) Specifically, how can you challenge yourself to extend fellowship to those who might not share the same values, interests, and ideas as you do?

_____

_____

_____

(d) How might such fellowship help lead others to a deeper relationship with Jesus and the Catholic Church?

_____

_____

_____

6

CONFLICT IN GALILEE
—MATTHEW 10-12—

By the end of chapter nine of Saint Matthew's Gospel, we see that Jesus has captivated everyone's attention and has won the hearts of the people. All of Israel is practically eating out of the palms of Jesus' hands . . . or so it appears at first glance.

We know that Jesus attracted large crowds from all over Palestine. Many traveled great distances to witness firsthand the exciting movement He was starting in Galilee (cf. Mt. 4:24-25). Just when His fame was reaching its peak, Jesus took the opportunity to lead large crowds of followers into the Galilean hillside to issue a startling summons which today is often referred to as "the Sermon on the Mount" (Mt. 5-7). In this famous discourse, Jesus set forth His kingdom agenda, and the crowds marveled at His words, recognizing Him as an authoritative teacher from God (cf. Mt. 7:28-29).

Then Jesus came down from that mountain to perform ten miracles, which drew even more fanfare. He cleansed lepers, calmed storms, and cured the sick. He healed a crippled man, forgave sins, and restored sight to the blind. However, these mighty actions in Galilee did not reach their climax until Jesus performed His tenth and greatest miracle of all: expelling a demon from a mute man (cf. Mt. 9:32-34).

The Exorcist

Why might an exorcism be considered His greatest miracle so far? In today's world, we do not often hear about exorcisms, let alone see them performed in the middle of our city streets. Yet for a first-century Jew, Jesus' driving out evil spirits would have been much more than just another exciting miracle.

When Jesus commanded a demon to leave an individual, He was not simply offering spiritual freedom to that particular person. Rather, His exorcisms sent a message that had great meaning for *all* the people of Israel: Jesus was fighting Israel's most important battle. He was building God's kingdom by driving out those demonic forces which had attacked the Israelite nation since the beginning of their history.

By expelling demons, Jesus boldly proclaimed His supreme authority as the Messiah-King. Although His other miraculous healings demonstrated His power over things of this world—such as diseases, physical ailments, and the skies and seas—Jesus' exorcisms showed that He had authority even over the spiritual realm. By issuing commands over the demons, Jesus manifested His power over the devil himself—the source of all evils in this world.

Such actions, indeed, stirred up hopes for the Messiah. In Jewish tradition, David's son, King Solomon, was known for his exorcisms and power over demons.[1] That's why some people responded to

---

[1] See Wisdom 7:17-20. See also the pseudepigraphic Testament of Solomon for an example of one strand of this tradition in Judiaism in *The Old Testament Pseudepigigrapha*, vol. 1, James H. Charlesworth, ed. (New York: Doubleday, 1983), 960-87.

Jesus' exorcisms by saying, "Can this be the Son of David?" (Mt. 12:23). And since the Jews expected the Messiah to be a descendent of David who would fight Israel's enemies, Jesus' mighty power over the greatest enemy, Satan, could have been interpreted as a messianic action.

So Jesus culminated His incredible tour of miraculous works in Galilee by expelling the demon from the mute man (cf. Mt. 9:32-33). This final climactic act captivated the crowds and left them completely astonished. They marveled at His ministry, saying "Never was anything like this seen in Israel" (Mt. 9:33). Jesus seems to have had the crowd in the palms of His hands.

However, not everyone was so impressed.

A Severe Accusation

Just when Jesus' movement seemed to be taking off with immense popularity, the Pharisees conspired to drag Him down and bring an end to the chaos and commotion His miracles had caused. They did not like what they were seeing in Galilee. Jesus claimed to be announcing the long-awaited kingdom that God had promised Israel, but He seemed to be establishing it in all the wrong ways and inviting all the wrong people. Sinners, prostitutes, and tax collectors were drawn into His table fellowship. He touched lepers and the diseased and spent time with other "untouchables." He even claimed to offer forgiveness of sins on His own authority apart from the established priesthood and the Temple system. "Who does this man think he is?" they would have asked themselves. Surely He could not have been from God if He was leading the people astray in these serious matters and creating further division among the people of Israel.

Yet the Pharisees could not deny Jesus' miraculous works. Everyone agreed that something supernatural was going on in Jesus' ministry. His works were so great that they must have been based on some higher spiritual power. The crowds attributed His mighty works to the power of God, but the Pharisees saw things rather differently. Since Jesus seemed to be leading the people away from God's Temple and the priesthood, and since He seemed to be associating with all the "untouchables," the Pharisees concluded that Jesus could not have been a man sent by God. He must have been a false prophet. They said that Jesus could control demons not by using the power of God, but by using a much darker force: "He casts out demons by the prince of demons" (Mt. 9:34). They were saying that the only reason Jesus could issue commands over the demons was because He Himself was in league with the prince of demons, Satan.

The Unforgivable Sin

This was the first seed of the Pharisees' quickly growing hostility toward Jesus. After this, they put Him under surveillance, watching every move He made, trying to find any small grounds on which they could criticize Him (Mt. 12:1-2). They tried to trap Him in His own words (Mt. 12:9-10). They even began plotting how to destroy Him (Mt. 12:14). The conflict escalated when Jesus expelled a demon from another man in Galilee. Once again, the people were amazed, but the Pharisees leveled a serious charge against Jesus: "It is only by Beelzebul, the prince of demons, that this man casts out demons" (Mt. 12:24).

At this point, the Pharisees had gone one step too far. Jesus shows them the severity of their accusation:

> But if it is by the Spirit of God that I cast out demons, then the kingdom of God has come upon you. . . . [E]very sin and blasphemy will be forgiven men, but the blasphemy against the Spirit will not be forgiven (Mt. 12:28, 31).

In other words, the Pharisees were blaspheming against God's own Spirit. If Jesus expelled demons by the power of the Holy Spirit, then the Pharisees were identifying that Holy Spirit of Jesus with the power of the devil. That is serious blasphemy. Once the Pharisees cut themselves off from the very source of salvation—Jesus and His Spirit—there was nothing more Jesus could do to work with them. That is why this sin cannot be forgiven. They had closed themselves off from the very Spirit by which Jesus offered forgiveness of sins.

The New Israel

In light of all this, Jesus knew that Israel needed a drastic change in leadership. He looked upon the crowds with great sadness, knowing that their own leaders would steer them away from Him.

> When he saw the crowds, he had compassion for them, because they were harassed and helpless, like sheep without a shepherd. Then he said to his disciples, "The harvest is plentiful, but the laborers

are few; pray therefore the Lord of the harvest to send out laborers into his harvest" (Mt. 9:36-38).

At this point in the ministry, Jesus did something He had not done before. After seeing that the people of Israel were like sheep without a shepherd and in desperate need of new leaders to guide them, Jesus turned to His close followers and singled out twelve men to be special leaders in His kingdom. This choosing of the twelve apostles marked a major shift in the ministry of Jesus.

More Than a Dozen

For the Jewish people, the number "12" was much more than a dozen. This sacred number brought to mind the twelve tribes of Israel which descended from the patriarch Jacob's twelve sons. These twelve tribes were the foundation stones upon which the nation of Israel had been built. Jesus drew upon this traditional symbolism. By going among His numerous followers and pulling twelve men aside to be His close associates, Jesus was sending an important message. Without saying a word, this action of choosing *twelve* men for special duty would have said, "The New Israel is *here!*" This action alone would have signaled that all the Jewish hopes for a renewed Israel were coming to fulfillment in Jesus' movement.

Therefore, when Jesus chose *twelve* apostles, He was symbolically expressing His intention to rebuild Israel—to reconstitute Israel around Himself with the apostles as the central leaders.

Building the Church

The word "apostle" means one who is sent. An apostle represents the one who sends, and shares in that person's authority. Saint Matthew's Gospel draws our attention to this point by an intricate display of literary art. Using a literary technique often called "chiasm," Matthew draws a number of parallels between what Jesus does in 9:35-38 and the mission He gives the apostles in 10:1-8. Jesus preaches the kingdom and heals the sick (9:35), and He sees the people are like sheep without a shepherd (9:36) and in need of laborers being sent out to them (9:38). All of this parallels in reverse order how Jesus sends the apostles out (10:5) as shepherds to the lost sheep of Israel (10:5) so that they may preach the Gospel of the kingdom and heal the sick just as Jesus did (10:7-8) (see diagram below).

— Apostolic Authority —
Matthew 9:35-10:8

(A) Jesus went about *preaching* the Gospel
of *the kingdom* and *healing* (9:35)
   (B) The people are like "*sheep
   without a shepherd*" (9:36)
      (C) Pray the Lord to *send out* laborers (9:38)
         (D) Jesus called *the twelve* disciples (10:1)
            (E) **Jesus gave the twelve authority (10:1)**
         (D) The names of "*the twelve*" (10:2)
      (C) Jesus *sent out* the twelve (10:5)
   (B) Jesus sent them to "the *lost sheep* of the
   house of Israel" (10:6)
(A) Apostles *preached* "*the kingdom* of heaven
is at hand" and *healed* (10:7-8)

In a chiasm's structure, what is most important is what is in the middle of all the parallels. That's what the narrator is trying to emphasize. At the center of these parallels in Matthew 9-10 is Jesus' choosing twelve apostles and *giving them authority* (10:1-2).

The theme of Jesus' authority is important for Matthew. In the opening chapter, he demonstrates Jesus' messianic authority as a true Son of David with His royal lineage traced in the genealogy. Matthew 3 shows Jesus' authority as the anointed King when the Spirit descends upon Him at the Jordan River. In Matthew 4, Jesus exercises His authority over the devil by defeating Him in the three desert temptations. In Matthew 5-7, Jesus establishes His authority in His teachings in the Sermon on the Mount, and in 8-9 He manifests His authority over the storms, the sea, disease, infirmities, and even demonic spirits. Matthew 1-9 is all about establishing Jesus' messianic authority through His words and deeds.

But in Matthew 10, *that very authority of Jesus is now given to the twelve apostles*. After the Pharisees accused Jesus of working with Satan (9:34), Jesus summoned the twelve apostles to be the leaders of the renewed Israel He was building.

Apostolic Authority

To emphasize the realism of the apostle's authority, Jesus went on to say to them, "He who receives you receives me" (Mt. 10:40). Invested with the authority of Jesus Himself, the apostles stand as representatives of Christ. Jesus was very clear: If you wanted to accept Him, you had to accept His apostles. This is why Catholics today are called to accept the shepherding of the modern-day apostles, the bishops, who stand as the successors of the original twelve (cf. Catechism, nos. 861-62). By receiving their guidance and teaching, we allow the Good Shepherd Himself to guide our lives through His representatives here on earth. All this can be seen in the prayer that priests recite in Masses for Feasts of the Apostles, as found in Catechism, no. 857:

You are the eternal Shepherd
who never leaves his flock untended.
Through the apostles
you watch over us and protect us always.
You made them shepherds of the flock
to share in the work of your Son. . . .

* * *

Questions for Discussion

1. Read Matthew 9:32-34 and 12:22-24.

(a) How do the crowds respond to Jesus' powerful exorcisms?

_____

_____

_____

(b) Why do Jesus' exorcisms stir up messianic hopes, with many saying "Can this be the Son of David?" (Mt. 12:23)?

_____

_____

_____

(c) How do the Pharisees respond to these exorcisms (9:34; 12:24)?

_____

_____

_____

(d) How do they try to discredit these powerful actions of Jesus?

_____

_____

_____

(e) Why do they do that?

_____

_____

2. Read Matthew 12:25-32.

(a) How does Jesus respond to the accusation of the Pharisees?

_____

_____

(b) Why does Jesus consider this accusation a blasphemy against the Holy Spirit?

_____

_____

3. Read Matthew 9:36-38. What does Jesus say about the contemporary leaders ("shepherds") of the Jewish people?

_____

_____

4. Read Matthew 9:36-10:8.

(a) How do these verses describe Jesus replacing Israel's religious leaders with leaders of His own? Note the parallels in the "chiastic" literary structure of this passage as illustrated on page 87.

_____

_____

(b) What is the symbolism of Jesus' choosing twelve apostles?

_____

_____

(c) How do these verses highlight Jesus' giving His royal authority to the apostles?

_____

_____

5. In light of Matthew 10, especially 10:40, respond to the following comment: "I just want to follow Jesus. I don't need a Church or any bishops. Jesus is my Good Shepherd. He will lead me."

_____

_____

_____

6. Is it sometimes difficult to view our bishops and priests as true representatives of Jesus? Why or why not?

_____

_____

_____

7. What would the Church be like if Jesus did not leave us with the apostles and their successors and did not give them authority to shepherd God's people?

_____

_____

_____

8. What can we do to cultivate greater respect and honor for these successors of the apostles, our bishops, in our daily lives?

_____

_____

_____

7

KEYS TO THE KINGDOM
—MATTHEW 13:1-16:19—

If you ever have the chance to visit the Vatican, go to the center of St. Peter's Basilica and just look up. You can't miss it. Some of the most important words Jesus ever spoke will stare down at you. Encircling the base of the dome, a line of three-foot-tall black letters pressed onto a gold background majestically spell out in Latin: *"You are Peter, and on this rock I will build my Church, and I will give you the keys of the kingdom of heaven."*

Even after visiting St. Peter's countless times during my years of study in Rome, I am still moved whenever I see these sacred words which Jesus spoke to Peter some 2,000 years ago. They not only mark a crucial point in Jesus' kingdom movement, but they are also commonly hailed as an important foundation for the role of the pope in Christ's kingdom today. Imagine what it would have been like to have been there during that pivotal conversation between Jesus and Peter. Let us go back to the city of Caesarea Philippi, where these words were spoken for the first time, so that we may hear them anew in the way the twelve apostles themselves might have originally understood them.

Who Do You Say That I Am?

So far, throughout most of Matthew's Gospel, we have been reading about how Jesus has been building His kingdom movement in the northern region of Israel known as Galilee. But in Matthew 16, His kingdom program takes a significant turn. In this scene, Jesus leads His twelve apostles north out of Galilee to a city called Caesarea Philippi. There, He initiated a conversation that would forever leave its mark on Christian history.

Jesus began by asking the apostles about the public's perception of Him and His ministry. What were the people saying about Him? The apostles reported that some thought Jesus was John the Baptist, while others thought He was Elijah, Jeremiah, or another one of the prophets. After hearing about what the crowds were saying, Jesus then turned to the twelve and posed the question on a more personal level: "But who do *you* say that I am?" (Mt. 16:15).

At this, Simon Peter took the lead and answered for them all: "You are the Christ, the Son of the living God" (Mt. 16:16). In other words, Peter was saying, "You are the anointed king we have been longing for. You are the one who will restore Israel and set us free." With these words, Peter became the first person in Matthew's Gospel explicitly to recognize Jesus as the long-awaited Messiah.

Jesus then responded to Peter's insight by blessing him and saying:

> Blessed are you, Simon Bar-Jona! For flesh and blood has not revealed this to you, but my Father who is in heaven. And I tell you, you are Peter, and on this rock I will build my church, and the powers of death shall not prevail against it. I will give you the keys of the kingdom of heaven, and whatever you bind on earth shall be bound in heaven, and whatever you loose on earth shall be loosed in heaven (Mt. 16:17-19).

These famous words serve as the foundation for understanding the role of the pope in the life of the Catholic Church. Yet, some may object that the passage doesn't appear to say anything about Peter's being an authoritative head of the Church and the Vicar of Christ, much less about his having successors who would continue this role of shepherding all Christians. Indeed, at first glance, the passage doesn't appear to portray Jesus as intending to start any type of ongoing papal lineage. However, when we read these words through the lenses of first-century Judaism, we see just how significant they would have been in the time of Jesus and how profoundly they might shed light on the Catholic understanding of the papacy today.

A New Name

The first thing about Jesus' words to Peter which would have captured the apostles' attention is the fact that Jesus changed Simon's name. This was not about giving Simon a new nickname. Rather, Jesus was giving him a new vocation. In Jewish tradition, a change in someone's name signified a change in the person. When God set certain people apart for special roles, He often gave them new names to signify their new purpose in the divine plan. For example, Abram's name is changed to Abraham (which means "father of a multitude") when Yahweh chose him to become the "father of a multitude of nations" (Gen. 17:5). Similarly, the patriarch Jacob's name was changed to Israel, highlighting the important role he would have as the father of the twelve tribes of the nation of Israel.

A new name signals a new mission. Thus, when Jesus gave Simon a new name, He was setting him apart from the other twelve apostles and bestowing on him a special function. This simple name change alone would have signaled to those apostles and other first-century Jews that Jesus was giving Peter an important role to play in His kingdom.

Like a Rock

The second element that would have stood out in Jesus' words to Peter would have been the new name itself. Jesus conferred on Simon the name "Peter"—*Kepha* in Jesus' language (Aramaic)—which means "rock." What is interesting is that *Kepha* was not commonly used as a proper name at that time. Although Peter is a common name found in many modern languages today, this was not the case in Jesus' day. Jesus took an ordinary word—rock—and used it to designate a human being, Simon Peter. The peculiarity of such an action would be similar to having your name changed to a word such as "stone" or "boulder" or some other word that is not normally used as a proper name.

What did Jesus mean when He called Simon by this non-name, "rock"? And what did He mean when He told him He would build His Church on him and the gates of death would not prevail against it?

A number of images come to mind. On a basic level, Jesus was simply saying that Peter will be rock-like: a durable, solid foundation giving the Church the firm and stable leadership it will need in the years ahead. On another level, Peter will be like Abraham who was described as the rock on which

God constructed and established the world (cf. Is. 51:1-2). These allusions point to the pivotal role Peter would play in God's plan for the Church. But there is another significant image Jesus probably was thinking of when He gave Simon the name "rock." And it is this image which has the most potential for illuminating the Catholic understanding of the papacy.

The Foundation Stone

The most important rock in all of Judaism was the "foundation stone" (Heb. *eben shetiyah*) in the Jerusalem Temple. According to Jewish tradition, this rock served not only as the base of the altar for sacrifice in the Temple, but also was associated with significant moments of salvation history. This rock was believed to be the site of creation and the foundation on which God built the world. It was the place where Abraham was willing to sacrifice his son Isaac to Yahweh. David dug down to this rock and made it the foundation for the Temple. And it was believed that this rock plugged up the waters of the abyss, the pit of death, and kept the demonic forces of deception and death sealed down below.[1]

These were vivid images that the Jews used to describe the profound reality of the Temple's relationship with the spiritual order. Simply put, the Temple was the sacred space where heaven and

---

[1] Thomas Fawcett, *Hebrew Myth and Christian Gospel* (London: SCM, 1973), 239-45; Zev Vilnay, *Legends of Jerusalem* (Philadelphia: Jewish Publication Society of America, 1973), 5-82; Roland de Vaux, *Ancient Israel* (New York: McGraw-Hill, 1965), 318-19; cf. Rev. 20.

earth met. To Jews, the Temple was the center of the universe, and the foundation stone was the point of intersection between the spiritual realm and the physical world.

Whatever one may make of these ancient Jewish traditions, what is important for us to note is how Jesus used these images when He referred to Simon as the *rock* upon which He would build His Church, and *the gates of death would not prevail against it*. In other words, Jesus was saying that Peter is like the Temple foundation stone. Just as God used the Temple rock to build the world and protect it from the chaotic waters and evil spirits underneath, so too God will use Peter to build the Church and protect His people from the powers of death.[2]

Keys to the Kingdom

After changing Simon's name to Peter, Jesus did something else that made Peter's important position in the kingdom even more obvious. Jesus gave Peter "the keys to the kingdom":

> I will give you the keys of the kingdom of heaven, and whatever you bind on earth shall be bound in heaven, and whatever you loose on earth shall be loosed in heaven (Mt. 16:19).

To understand the royal symbolism of the keys given to Peter, we need to see how they were used in the Davidic kingdom of the Old Testament.

---

[2] Fawcett, 244-45; de Vaux, 318-19.

The key of the house of David symbolized the administrative authority of the "master of the palace"—the king's highest ranking official in the royal court. Similar to prime minister-like positions in other ancient near-eastern kingdoms, the master of the palace in the Davidic dynasty shared in the king's own authority, governed in the king's name, and acted for him in his absence.[3]

Isaiah 22 describes the promotion of a man named Eliakim to this most prestigious office. As master of the palace, Eliakim handled the day-to-day affairs of the kingdom for the king. He wore a royal robe and exercised authority, ruling as a father figure over the people of Judah. To symbolize the unique authority he held, he was given the key of the house of David. Holding the key to the kingdom, this new master of the palace was described as "a peg in a sure place" and "a throne of honor" to his father's house (Is. 22:15-23).

This is the royal imagery Jesus was alluding to when He gave Peter the keys to the kingdom. Jesus was saying that Peter will be the new "master of the palace" in the kingdom He was building. Since the keys symbolized how the Davidic king vested the prime minister with his very authority, Jesus, in giving Peter the keys to the kingdom, was saying: "You, Peter, will be the prime minister in my kingdom. You will be vested with my very authority so that you can shepherd the people in my name."

---

[3] de Vaux, 130.

What About Succession?

Up to this point, we have seen that Jesus certainly singled out Peter for having a unique role in His kingdom. Peter underwent a name change signifying his special vocation. He was the foundation rock for the Church, keeping even the powers of evil at bay. And he was given the keys to the kingdom, designating him as the prime minister, ruling with Jesus' authority in the Church. Matthew's Gospel clearly shows us that Peter was elevated to a preeminent position of authority in Christ's kingdom.

But where do Catholics get the idea of an ongoing papacy? All that we can conclude from the passage so far is that *Peter* was given this special authoritative position. It is one thing to say that Jesus established Peter as the head of the Church, but it is another thing to claim that Jesus intended for there to be successors to Peter's office throughout the centuries down to the present pope today. Where does Matthew 16 mention anything about this special authority being *passed on to successors?*

The answer again lies in the keys. Isaiah 22 tells how Eliakim was replacing the previous master of the palace, a man named Shebna. To symbolize the transfer of the office from Shebna to Eliakim, Eliakim was given the key to the house of David (cf. Is. 22:22). It is important to note that Eliakim was assuming an office that continued from generation to generation. And it was the handing on of the keys which symbolized the transfer of the prime minister's office to his successor. Thus, the notion of succession was built right into the image of the keys.

So when Jesus gave Peter the keys, He was entrusting His authority not only to Peter, but also to all his successors. Jesus was saying something like, "I give this authority not only to you, Peter, but also to all those who come after you in this office." Therefore, the keys were not meant to be kept by Peter alone, but were intended to be passed on to Peter's successors just as they were passed on from one prime minister to the next in the Davidic kingdom of old.

This is why the Catholic Church has always taught that Peter's successor—the pope—serves as the "Vicar of Christ" and preeminent shepherd of God's people (cf. Catechism, no. 882). As the modern-day successor of Peter and bearer of "the keys," the pope stands as the current prime minister in Christ's kingdom. Sharing in all the prerogatives of this royal office, the pope is the King's representative. As the prime minister, he is vested with Jesus' authority and leads God's people in Christ's name. And like the prime minister Eliakim, who was a father to the people in the kingdom of David (cf. Is. 22:21), the pope leads us as our "Holy Father" in the New Covenant kingdom of Jesus, the Church.

* * *

Questions for Discussion

1. Read Matthew 16:13-19. Consider the significance of Simon's name being changed to Peter.

(a) First, what is the importance of name changes in the Bible?

_____

_____

(b) Can you think of any examples from the Scriptures when God changed a person's name at an important turning point in his or her life?

_____

_____

(c) What does Peter's new name mean?

_____

_____

(d) What rock might Jesus be referring to when He calls Peter the rock upon which He will build the Church and the gates of death shall not prevail against it?

_____

_____

(e) What might this say about Peter's role in the Church?

_____

_____

2. In addition to changing his name to Peter, Jesus also gave Peter "the keys of the kingdom of heaven"

(Mt. 16:19). To grasp the significance of these keys, read Isaiah 22:15-23. This passage describes how the Lord was going to remove a man named Shebna from his office as the master of the palace in the Davidic kingdom. This was a prime minister-like office which ruled over the people with the king's very authority. The passage goes on to tell how the keys to the kingdom will be transferred from Shebna to a successor, a man named Eliakim.

(a) In light of Isaiah 22:15-23, what did it mean to have the keys to the kingdom in the Davidic dynasty? What does this passage say about the authority of the person with the keys?

_____

_____

_____

_____

(b) How might this background shed light on Peter's role in Christ's kingdom?

_____

_____

3. Respond to the following question: "Jesus might have given Peter a unique authoritative position in the kingdom, but the Scriptures nowhere teach that this position was meant to be passed on to *successors*. Where do the Scriptures say anything about an ongoing papacy with Peter having successors?"

_____

_____

_____

4. Read Catechism, nos. 880-82. How do people today view the pope? Why might some people have difficulty accepting the pope as Christ's representative ruler and head of the Church?

_____

_____

5. How might the biblical foundations for the papacy discussed in this chapter make it easier for people to understand the essential role of the pope in Christ's kingdom?

_____

_____

6. What can we do to promote a greater respect and love for the pope as our Holy Father in our own lives and in the lives of others?

_____

_____

8

THE SECRET OF THE MESSIAH
—MATTHEW 16:20-21:11—

"Ssshhhh. . . . Don't tell anyone yet!"
That is basically what Jesus told the twelve apostles once they realized that He was the Messiah. In
the last chapter, we saw that Simon Peter was the
first person to explicitly declare that Jesus was the
long-awaited Davidic king. In dramatic fashion,
Jesus praised Simon for his insight and gave him a
preeminent office in His Church, as symbolized by
the keys to the kingdom. Yet, at this exciting
moment, Jesus did something which on the surface
doesn't seem to make much sense: "Then he strictly
charged the disciples to tell no one that he was the
Christ" (Mt. 16:20).

Why would Jesus be so secretive? Didn't He want
people to know His messianic identity? Jesus' push
for secrecy is understandable when we consider the
first-century Jewish context. Recall how "messiah"
means "anointed one," referring to the anointing of a
king. Thus, if word got out that He was explicitly
claiming to be the Messiah-King, Jesus would have
attracted the wrong sort of attention. Given the political and militaristic emphasis attached to the Jewish
messianic hopes in Jesus' day, such a public procla-
mation of His messiahship might have put Him in a
dangerous situation. Anyone gathering a large group
of followers and then claiming to be their anointed
king certainly would have been considered a threat
to the foreign powers that ruled the land. In fact, the

last time would-be messiahs had entered the scene
in Palestine, just one generation before Jesus, their
movements had been swiftly squashed by Herod and
the Roman armies, and the leaders had been execut-
ed. Jesus was not ready for that quite yet. Although
His time would come soon, He still had some work
to do in His kingdom-building plan.

No Coattails

One such task involved redefining the popular
notion of messiahship, divesting it of the political
and militaristic connotations it carried in many sec-
tors of first-century Judaism. Many Jews in this time
longed for a political messiah because they thought
their problem centered primarily on the Roman
occupation. Jesus, however, knew that Israel's problem was much deeper. He knew Israel was suffering
from an oppressive force that was much more devastating than Roman soldiers or Caesar's taxes. The
real problem facing Israel—and the rest of the
world—was sin. Oppressive regimes, violent govern-
ments, and unjust economic structures were only
symptoms of the much more serious illness of
human sinfulness. Jesus knew that the only way the
external societal structures of Israel would be
changed was through an internal transformation,
beginning right in their own hearts. Political, social,
and economic liberation would only be accomplished through the ultimate liberation from sin.
And that is the type of freedom Jesus offered Israel
as the Messiah-King.

He had much work to do, however, in explaining
His mission as the Messiah, and He began with His

own disciples. Even they were not immune to the popular way of envisioning the Messiah primarily through political and militaristic lenses. With this perspective, imagine what they were thinking once they realized that their own leader was the Messiah-King. What exhilaration and anticipation must have filled their hearts once they knew that their Jesus was the one spoken of by the prophets—the one who would rise victoriously over Israel's enemies and restore the kingdom. Since Jesus had invited them to be co-leaders of His movement, the apostles probably hoped to obtain high-ranking offices once the kingdom was established.

Much to their dismay, Jesus had another type of kingdom in mind, one that He wanted His apostles to understand. Notice how, immediately after Peter's recognition that Jesus was the Messiah, Our Lord painted a stark picture of what kind of Messiah He was to be. In the very first verse after the scene of Peter's profession of faith, Matthew shows us how Jesus began telling the disciples about His upcoming death in Jerusalem:

> *From that time* Jesus began to show his disciples that he must go to Jerusalem and suffer many things from the elders and chief priests and scribes, and be killed, and on the third day be raised (Mt. 16:21).

Think of what a shock this must have been to the apostles. What kind of Messiah was *this?* How could the Messiah be killed? Even Peter—who was just praised for recognizing Jesus as the promised Messiah—could not comprehend the idea of the Messiah-King's dying at the hands of his enemies: "God forbid, Lord! This shall never happen to you" (Mt. 16:22).

This was the first time Jesus spoke explicitly to the apostles about His future death, and this difficult conversation could not have come at a more strategic time. Now that it was clear to His disciples that He was indeed the Messiah, Jesus needed to stress to them that His royal reign would be established not on the battlefield or in the political arena, but through His death on the Cross. And right away He warned the apostles to think twice before vying for offices in His kingdom. Far from being able to ride the Messiah's coattails into powerful positions in the kingdom, the apostles faced a radical challenge if they wished to participate in Jesus' reign:

> If any man would come after me, let him deny himself and take up his cross and follow me. For whoever would save his life will lose it, and whoever loses his life for my sake will find it (Mt. 16:24-25).

Here we see that the pathway to Jesus' kingdom is not military muscle or monarchical might, but sacrificial love and service.

Journey Toward Jerusalem

From this point on, Jesus' movement in Galilee picked up a new focus. In Israel's history, Jewish kings reigned from Jerusalem. Therefore, if Jesus was the Messiah-King, He must go to the capital city to be enthroned. This is why Jesus begins speaking of His death in Jerusalem and taking His movement in the direction of the holy city.

Along the way, we see him continuing to redefine the notion of the Messiah and the kingdom for His apostles, emphasizing how His reign will be quite different from the world's view of governing authority. In Matthew 18:1-4, Jesus extols certain qualities that few government leaders would see as essential to their authority. For Jesus, humility and childlikeness are fundamental characteristics of His kingdom: "Whoever humbles himself like this child, he is the greatest in the kingdom" (Mt. 18:4). Another feature of the kingdom of Jesus is forgiveness and mercy. Peter asks how many times he should forgive someone who harms him. "Seven times?" Peter asks. Jesus said to him, "I do not say to you seven times, but seventy times seven" (Mt. 18:22). This kingdom of forgiveness would have stood in contrast with many Jewish groups that wanted revenge on their pagan enemies.

Yet even after Jesus spoke about His upcoming death and the self-sacrifice, humility, and forgiveness that are hallmarks of His kingdom, the apostles still did not get it. An episode in Matthew 20 illustrates how the kingdom was still understood primarily in political categories. As Jesus and His followers were drawing nearer to Jerusalem, the mother of James and John approached Jesus on her knees with an amazing request: "Command that these two sons of mine may sit, one at your right hand and one at your left, in your kingdom" (Mt. 20:21). Not understanding the true nature of the kingdom and the price Jesus would pay for it, the mother of these two apostles asked Jesus to give her sons the first places in His kingdom.

Jesus uses this as another opportunity to emphasize what His kingdom is really all about. He turns to
the apostles and asks, "Are you able to drink the cup
that I am to drink?" referring to His imminent suffering and death (Mt. 20:22). Jesus then contrasts
His kingdom with the kingdoms of the world:

> You know that the rulers of the Gentiles lord it over
> them, and their great men exercise authority over
> them. It shall not be so among you; but whoever
> would be great among you must be your servant,
> and whoever would be first among you must be
> your slave; even as the Son of man came not to be
> served but to serve, and to give his life as a ransom
> for many (Mt. 20:25-28).

Humility, service, forgiveness, and sacrificial
love. Jesus constantly returned to these themes in
His teachings about the kingdom on the way to
Jerusalem. Although many Jews wanted a military
king who would free them from the pagan nations
oppressing them, Jesus knew that the solution to
the sin of the Gentiles was not destroying their
armies, but converting their hearts. Indeed, this was
Israel's mission from the very beginning. God called
their founding father Abraham and his descendants
(the Israelites) to be the instrument for bringing
blessing to a broken world. Israel was not called to
fight off the world, but to be its light. And Jesus
knew it would only be through serving the Gentiles,
forgiving them, and loving them that even the most
wicked of nations could be won over to worship the
one true God.

The Coming of the King

Finally, Jesus arrives at Jerusalem (cf. Mt. 21:1-11). Here we come to a famous scene from the Gospels with which Catholics are quite familiar. The drama of "Palm Sunday" is relived every year in the liturgy when Catholics carry branches and process into church, recalling Jesus' procession into Jerusalem with the people greeting him as "the Son of David" and waving palm branches like they did when Judas Maccabeus freed the city from the Syrians (cf. 2 Mac. 10:7).

Notice how the people of Jerusalem gave Jesus a royal greeting. They, in a sense, rolled out a royal carpet for their monarch by spreading out branches and their garments on the ground where Jesus would walk—a custom ancient Jews did for kings in the Davidic monarchy (cf. 2 Kings 9:13). They called Jesus "the Son of David" and sang "Blessed is he who comes in the name of the Lord! Hosanna in the highest!" (Mt. 21:9).

One question we should ask is, "Why did the people give Jesus this royal treatment?" If Jesus instructed His disciples to keep His messianic identity somewhat quiet, why did the people come out to honor Him as their king entering the capital city? It all has to do with a donkey.

Royal Treatment

It is significant that Jesus deliberately chose to enter Jerusalem riding on a donkey. This little detail alone tells us something important is about to happen. Nowhere else in the Gospel do we read about Jesus traveling on an animal. Everywhere else He traveled,

Jesus went on foot over land, and on boat over sea (and one time on foot over the sea when He walked on the water!)—but we never find Him riding on a donkey, or any other animal, except when He enters Jerusalem. Why this new mode of transportation?

A key prophecy of Zechariah helps to illuminate this scene. Zechariah 9:9-10 foretells how the Messiah will enter Jerusalem riding on a young donkey:

> Rejoice greatly, O daughter of Zion!
>   Shout aloud, O daughter of Jerusalem!
> *Lo, your king comes to you;*
>   triumphant and victorious is he,
> *humble and riding on an ass,*
>   *on a colt the foal of an ass. . . .*
> [H]e shall command peace to the nations;
> his dominion shall be from sea to sea,
>   and from the River to the ends of the earth.

Jesus deliberately chose to enter Jerusalem in this way in order to bring to mind Zechariah 9:9, a passage which the Jews probably knew very well. This prophecy summed up their hopes for the Messiah—the one for whom they waited their whole lives, the one who would rescue them from their oppressors. By riding into the holy city on a young donkey, Jesus, without saying a single word, was shouting out, "I am the Messiah-King coming to be enthroned in Jerusalem!" If there were any question about Jesus' messianic claims, this action would have removed all doubt. Zechariah 9:9 was being fulfilled right there before their eyes. In this action, Jesus boldly and explicitly proclaimed that He was the Messiah. Certainly this was cause for great rejoicing and celebration.

We saw earlier that if Jesus were to publicly pro-
claim His messianic identity, He would quickly find
Himself in big trouble. With Herod and the Romans
ready to crush any rising revolutionaries or rival
kings, a claim to messiahship would likely bring about
an early end to His ministry and His very life. But
after having laid the foundations for His kingdom,
Jesus was now ready to make that bold move of
announcing Himself to be Israel's long-awaited
Messiah-King. He had invested the apostles with His
authority (Mt. 10), established Peter as the prime
minister in the kingdom (Mt. 16), and trained His
disciples on the true nature of the kingdom He was
building (Mt. 16-20). They would continue His work
after His departure from this world. Now at
Jerusalem, Jesus rode into the holy city on a donkey,
symbolically declaring Himself to be the Messiah . . .
and in a few days He would pay the price.

✝   ✝   ✝

Questions for Discussion

1. Read Matthew 16:20. Why do you think Jesus wanted to keep His messianic identity secret?

_____

_____

2. Read Matthew 16:21, 24-28. Why does Jesus begin talking about His upcoming death in Jerusalem *now*? What happened in the previous scene with Peter's profession of faith that made Jesus want to stress the suffering and death He would endure?

_____

_____

3. What do the following passages say about Jesus' vision for authority in His kingdom?

Matthew 16:24-28

_____

_____

Matthew 18:1-4

_____

_____

Matthew 18:21-22

_____

_____

Matthew 20:20-28

_____

_____

4. How does this view of authority differ from modern-day views of power? Which is more effective? Why?

_____

_____

_____

_____

_____

5. Based on Jesus' teachings about leadership in His kingdom, how can you be a more effective leader for Christ . . .

(a) in your family?

_____

_____

(b) at work?

_____

_____

(c) in your parish?

_____

_____

(d) in your community?

_____

_____

6. Read Matthew 21:1-11.

(a) Now read 1 Kings 1:38-40, which describes King Solomon's coronation, and Zechariah 9:9-11. In light of these passages, what is Jesus symbolically announcing when He enters Jerusalem riding on a donkey?

_____

_____

_____

(b) How do the people respond to Jesus' arrival? In what ways do they treat him like a king?

_____

_____

(c) Why does Jesus now feel free to publicly announce His messiahship with full force?

_____

_____

(d) What will happen to Him later that week as a result of this announcement?

_____

_____

9

Jesus, the Temple, and the End Times
—Matthew 21:12-25:46—

Imagine gazing upon a building which makes up about one-fourth of an entire city and occupies an area equivalent to thirty-five football fields. That's what Jewish pilgrims would see when they approached the gigantic Temple to worship the one, true God. It has been said that the Temple in Jerusalem was not just a large building in one part of the city. It was more like "Jerusalem was a Temple with a city around it!"[1]

The immensity of the Temple is not surprising, considering the fact that this sacred building—and all that it stood for—was the very center of Jewish life. This was the place where the God of the universe came to meet His chosen people. The Jews believed that the Temple actually housed God's awesome presence in its innermost chamber called the Holy of Holies. As the connecting point between heaven and earth, the Temple came to be known as "the naval of the world" and the center of the whole cosmos—the place where God's holiness radiated outward to the rest of creation.[2]

Indeed, the Jews believed their Temple to be a symbol for the entire world, a miniature replica of the universe made in architecture. What went on in the

---

[1] N.T. Wright, *The Original Jesus* (Oxford: Lion Publishing, 1996), 57-58.
[2] Marcus J. Borg, *Conflict, Holiness and Politics in the Teachings of Jesus* (Harrisburg, PA: Trinity Press International, 1998), 75-76.

sacred space of the Temple—sacrifice, worship, and the dwelling of God's presence—was a reminder for God's people of the praise and worship that should resound from all corners of the world.

In addition to being the focal point for worship and sacrifice, the Temple also served as the center for Jewish government, their judicial system, and their trade and economics. Thus, the Temple in Jerusalem was the first-century Jewish version of the Vatican, White House, Supreme Court, and Wall Street all wrapped into one. In short, the Temple was everything to the Jews. It stood out as the number one symbol for Jewish national identity.

So why did Jesus go in there and turn everything upside down?

Kingship and the Temple

The great Jewish kings exercised their reign through building or purifying the Temple. David came up with the idea for the first Temple. His son Solomon built it and dedicated it to the Lord. Great reformer kings such as Hezekiah and Josiah built their renewals around restoring the Temple. Judas Maccabeus won a century-long dynasty for his family because he cleansed the Temple from the pagan idolatry of the Syrians. Herod, who was not a true Jew and received his throne from the Romans, tried to legitimize his claim to kingship in Judea by rebuilding the Temple in great splendor. As we can see, kingship and the Temple went hand in hand in Israel's history.

One of the first things Jesus did when He arrived in Jerusalem was to enter the Temple. There He performed a powerful, symbolic action, which must be understood in light of Israel's prophetic tradition. Let us recall how Israel's prophets often communicated more with their actions than they did with their words. For example, in a time when the Temple elders were corrupt and the Jerusalem leaders were leading the people away from God's covenant, the prophet Jeremiah took a clay jar to the Temple priests, smashed it in front of them, and explained that what he just did with the jar symbolized what God would do with Jerusalem and the Temple because of their unfaithfulness (cf. Jer. 19:10-11). Jesus performed a similar act of judgment on the Temple when He overturned the tables of the money-changers and prevented anyone from buying and selling in the Temple courts.

Turning Everything Upside Down

When Jews traveled to Jerusalem for Temple worship, they needed to present the Temple priests with pure animals to be offered in sacrifice. Rather than carry cattle, sheep, or goats with them on a long journey, they generally bought their animals in Jerusalem. But to make this purchase, they needed to obtain the local currency for doing business at the Temple. Hence, they went to the money-changers' tables in the Temple courts to exchange their money for the right coinage. This was the first step pilgrims would take when they wanted to offer sacrifices.

By turning all the money-changers' tables upside down, Jesus prevented anyone from getting the proper coinage. With no currency exchange, animals could not be bought and, consequently, sacrifices could not be offered. Thus, in one broad stroke, Jesus put a stop to the entire Temple system for a few hours—prefiguring how all sacrifices would soon cease and the Temple in Jerusalem would be destroyed forever. Like Jeremiah who smashed the clay jar, Jesus' actions symbolized how the Jerusalem Temple would soon be destroyed by the Romans.

Breaking Down Walls

But why would Jesus condemn the Temple in this way? He explained His actions in the Temple by saying: "It is written, 'My house shall be called a house of prayer'; but you make it a den of robbers" (Mt. 21:13). First, Jesus quoted a passage from Isaiah 56, which should be read in its context. Isaiah 56 emphasized the universality of God's plan of salvation. It described how the Lord will gather even the Gentiles—the non-Jews—to Himself in the New Covenant era. In fact, the verse which Jesus quoted tells how He wants peoples from all nations to come to the Jerusalem Temple to worship Him: "[M]y house shall be called a house of prayer for all peoples" (Is. 56:7). Thus, Jesus quoted Isaiah 56 in order to recall Israel's mission to gather the nations together to worship the one true God.

However, rather than being a source of bringing in the Gentiles, the Temple in Jesus' day had become a source of keeping them out. No other institution stood out more as Israel's national identity marker, setting the Jews apart from the non-Jews. An inscription over the entryway to the Temple's inner courts made the point crystal clear: "No alien may enter within the barrier and wall around the Temple. Whoever is caught is alone responsible for the death which follows."[3]

Many interpret Jesus' statement about the Temple's becoming a "den of robbers" to be a denunciation of the commercialism which supposedly had entered God's holy house. However, *lestai*, the Greek word in the New Testament text, often translated "robbers" or "thieves," actually referred to much more than swindling merchants who exploited people economically. Rather, it referred to those who killed and destroyed while stealing. In the first century, the word *lestai* could be used to describe revolutionaries who wanted to take up arms against the Romans. Indeed, the Temple had become a focal point for Israel's resistance to Roman domination.[4]

Thus, when Jesus said, "You made this house a den of *lestai*," He was not primarily condemning economic exploitation. Rather, He was saying that the Jerusalem Temple was meant to be a light to the nations, a house of prayer for all peoples, but its leaders had made it a point of focus for resistance.

Second Coming

Jesus' frustrations with the Temple are evident when He exited the building with His apostles another time later in the week. As they gazed at the magnificent structures of the Temple, the apostles marveled at the beautiful edifice, which was one of the most impressive buildings of the ancient world. In the midst of their amazement, Jesus told them that this

---

[3] *Ibid.*, 76.
[4] *Ibid.*, 185-89.

massive building soon would be destroyed: "Truly, I say to you, there will not be left here one stone upon another, that will not be thrown down" (Mt. 24:2).

The apostles asked Him when this would take place and what would be the signs. Jesus responded with a lengthy apocalyptic discourse in which He spoke of wars, earthquakes, famines, the sun and moon darkening, stars falling from the sky, and the need to flee from the city to the mountains. He concluded this discourse by giving a timetable for when all this would occur: "Truly, I say to you, this generation will not pass away till all these things take place" (Mt. 24:34).

Many interpret Jesus' words in this passage as referring primarily to His second coming at the end of time. However, there is one problem with this interpretation: Jesus said these events would take place *within a generation*. Yet we know the stars in fact did not fall, and the sun and moon continue to brighten the sky. So did Jesus get the timing of the world's end wrong?

Falling Stars

Here we must see that Jesus was using traditional Jewish apocalyptic imagery, which in the Old Testament was not meant to portray the physical destruction of the world and the end of the space-time universe. Rather, Israel's prophets used such cataclysmic language to describe the fall of great empires, powers, and institutions that were corrupt and hostile to God's people. Cosmic metaphors fittingly depicted how God would rid the world of those wicked rulers, bringing their reigns to an end.

For example, when speaking about the judgment that would fall upon a wicked Jerusalem, the prophet Ezekiel used the imagery of famine, pestilence, and wars, and he warned the Jews to escape to the mountains. He used such language to describe the horror Jerusalem would face when the Babylonians would soon come in and crush the city (cf. Ezek. 7:14-16). Similarly, the prophets Jeremiah and Zechariah called for Jews to flee from Babylon on the day when Yahweh would liberate and vindicate His people by demolishing the Babylonian empire (cf. Jer. 50:8, 28; Zech. 2:6-8). Other prophets used the image of earthquakes to depict great nations which soon would tumble to the ground. The cosmic imagery of the sun and moon darkening and stars falling from the sky described how Israel's enemies, such as Babylon and Egypt, would lose their strength and fall from power (cf. Is. 13:1, 10; 14:12; Ezek. 32:7-8; Joel 2:10).

Israel's prophets routinely spoke this way to portray God's intervention in the history of the world's great powers as dramatic, "earth-shaking" events. Although this prophetic imagery was not meant to describe the end of *the* world, it certainly emphasized the imminent end of a world—the end of the Babylonian world, the Egyptian world, and the world of other powers who opposed God's people.

Standing in that same prophetic tradition, Jesus spoke of famines, wars, earthquakes, people fleeing, the sun and moon darkening, and stars falling from the sky. And He did so in the context of His predicting the destruction of the Temple (cf. Mt. 24:2). Like the prophets before Him, Jesus employed these catastrophic images to prophetically foretell how God was coming in judgment on Israel's enemies. However, Jesus did so with an ironic twist. This time, the enemies of God's people were not Babylon, Assyria, Egypt, or even Rome, but rather the leaders in Jerusalem and the Temple! God's judgment now would fall upon the Temple leaders who had become corrupt and were leading the people away from the true Messiah-King, Jesus.

The End of a World

Jesus prophesied that the Temple would be destroyed within one generation, and His prediction was right on the money. About forty years after Jesus spoke these words, Roman troops raided Jerusalem, burned down the city, and destroyed the Temple in 70 A.D.—all taking place within a generation, just as He had foretold.

Think about what the end of the Temple would mean. We earlier saw how the Temple summed up Israel's entire life and covenant with God. Practically all aspects of Israel's relationship with Yahweh in the Old Covenant were related to the Temple. Thus, insofar as the Temple summed up the Old Covenant, the end of the Temple would symbolize the end of the Old Covenant world. Indeed, that is exactly what we have seen Jesus bringing about: the end of the old, so He could usher in the new.

Furthermore, there may be a secondary sense in which Jesus' words can be seen as pointing not only to the destruction of Jerusalem, but also to the end of the physical world. Recall how the Jews viewed their Temple as the center of the universe and as a symbol for the entire cosmos. As such, the destruction of the

Temple might signify what the end of the world may be like. While Jesus' words point primarily to the demise of the Temple in 70 A.D., they also prefigure what could happen to the entire cosmos at the end of time.[5]

* * *

---

[5] George Montague notes how the destruction of the Temple and the end of the world could have been closely associated in Jesus' mind, "for Jews considered the Temple to be one of the foundations of the world, and the end of the one would be the end of the other." George T. Montague, S.M., *Companion God* (New York: Paulist Press, 1989), 262.

Questions for Discussion

1. Recalling our reflections in this chapter, what did the Jews believe about their Temple? In what ways was the Temple the center of their lives?

_____

_____

_____

2. Read Matthew 21:12-13.

(a) What was the purpose of the money-changers in the Temple? Why were they so important for the Temple's sacrificial system?

_____

_____

_____

(b) What was Jesus symbolically saying about the Temple when He overturned the money-changers' tables?

_____

_____

3. Consider Jesus' explanation for His actions in Matthew 21:13. If the Temple was God's house and the very center of Israel's life, why was Jesus condemning it?

_____

_____

4. In His discourse in Matthew 24:4-35, Jesus uses an array of cataclysmic images such as earthquakes, fleeing to the mountains, and the sun, moon, and stars darkening to describe some type of earth-shattering event. To understand the event to which Jesus was referring in these verses, consider the following questions:

(a) Matthew 24:1-2 sets the context for His apocalyptic discourse in the rest of the chapter. What is Jesus speaking about in Matthew 24:1-2?

_____

_____

(b) How do the Old Testament prophets use similar cosmic imagery in the following passages:

Isaiah 13:1, 9-10

_____

_____

Isaiah 14:4, 12

_____

_____

Ezekiel 32:1-2,7-8

_____

_____

Is this Old Testament prophetic imagery of the sun, moon, and stars darkening and falling from the sky primarily used to describe the end of the physical world, or God's coming in judgment upon particular nations?

_____

_____

(c) In light of this background, how should we interpret Jesus' use of similar language in Matthew 24:29? Who might God be coming to judge?

_____

_____

_____

(d) According to verse 34, when does Jesus say all these events will take place?

_____

_____

(e) Certainly, the world was not destroyed in that time period. So what was Jesus referring to? What was actually destroyed within that time period?

_____

_____

10

THE TRIAL OF THE KING
—MATTHEW 26:1-27:26—

Jesus' actions were bound to get Him in trouble sooner or later. In those days, someone couldn't just ride into Jerusalem, signal messianic fulfillment, and then expect to go unnoticed. Nor could one march into the holy Temple, condemn it, and predict its destruction without attracting the wrong sort of attention.

Although the crowds rejoiced at His coming to Jerusalem and welcomed Him as a king (cf. Mt. 21:1-11), Jesus must have made the Jewish authorities anxious. How could they get excited about a growing movement which challenged their authority and shook the nation's very identity? In their eyes, Jesus' entire movement stood in opposition to the Temple and the Torah. They saw Him leading the people away from God's holy house and from God's sacred law. They would ask: "How could this man be the Messiah? He eats with sinners, disregards the purity laws, and forgives sins on His own authority. And who does He think He is condemning God's holy Temple in this way?" They probably saw Jesus as a false prophet, leading the people astray. Therefore, He had to be stopped (cf. Deut. 13:1-5).

Wicked Tenants

During that tumultuous week in Jerusalem, Jesus seemed to be aware that His days were numbered. He even told parables which prefigured His upcoming death. For example, Jesus told a story about a landowner who let his vineyard be run by tenants.

When the landowner sent his servants to collect the fruit from the land, the tenants killed each of the servants one by one. Finally, the landowner decided to send his own son, saying, "They will respect my son." But the tenants murdered even the son. In the end, the tenants were driven off the land and killed for their wickedness (cf. Mt. 21:33-46).

Jesus told this story to the chief priests (cf. Mt. 21:23). Since He was building on a traditional Jewish story (taken from Isaiah 5), they would have recognized that the vineyard represented Israel and the landowner was God.

But Jesus adds His own twist to the story. He introduces the tenants who are in charge of the land, but have not yielded fruit for the landowner. These tenants represent the leaders of Israel, who have not been good shepherds for the people. He also includes the servants who were sent by the landowner to collect the fruit. These servants represent the prophets whom God sent to challenge Israel's leaders to be fruitful and to live out the calling to be light to the nations. Finally, He introduced the landowner's son. Though Israel rejected all of the prophets, God is now sending one last messenger—one who surpasses all the others. This time, God is sending His own Son, Jesus. Sadly, the leaders of Israel will kill Him, too.

After hearing the story, the chief priests realized that Jesus was speaking about them (cf. Mt. 21:45). They were like the tenants who had rejected God's prophets, and now they were about to kill the landowner's son. As a result, they would be punished like the tenants in the story. Jesus said to them, "Therefore I tell you, the kingdom of God will be taken away from you and given to a nation producing the fruits of it" (Mt. 21:43).

On Trial

With the help of the Apostle Judas, the chief priests and elders eventually arrested Jesus at night and brought Him to trial before the high priest, Caiaphas, and the other Jewish leaders in Jerusalem (cf. Mt. 26:57-68). First, the council tried to gather false testimony against Him. Then, He was accused of condemning the Temple. All the while, Jesus remained silent, offering no defense. Only once did He speak, and that was when the high priest stood up and commanded Jesus by oath to tell him one thing: "Tell us if you are the Messiah!" At that, Jesus finally responded and, in two short sentences, He turned their whole worldview completely inside out: "You have said so. But I tell you, hereafter you will see the Son of man seated at the right hand of Power, and coming on the clouds of heaven" (Mt. 26:64).

At this, the high priest tore his robes in disgust and accused Jesus of blasphemy, and the council members slapped Him, spat on Him, and condemned Him to death. A harsh punishment for two little sentences! What did Jesus say that got Him into so much trouble? Why did the chief priests become so infuriated at these words? Why were these the words that sent Jesus off to the Romans?

Night Vision

In speaking of the Son of man coming on the clouds of heaven, Jesus was alluding to a famous prophecy in the Book of Daniel. The prophet Daniel had a dream—perhaps it could be considered a night-mare—about four dreadful beasts who were devouring God's people: a lion with wings, a man-eating bear, a four-headed leopard, and a most fierce beast with ten horns and iron teeth. Each beast represented four powerful Gentile kingdoms which waged war on the Jewish people. Suddenly, a mysterious human fig-ure appeared in the dream—"one like a son of man" (Dan. 7:13). The beasts were then destroyed, while the Son of man was taken up to the throne of God and given authority to rule over all the nations.

This was a prophecy of great hope. In the vision, the Son of man represents God's faithful people who had suffered under one severe Gentile regime after another. But in the end, the Son of man eventually would be rescued by God and would be vindicated as the enemies of Israel were defeated. God's people finally would be freed, and they would share in His reign over all the nations.

The Chief Beasts

In His trial before the high priest, Jesus evoked this vision of Daniel and associated Himself with the Son of man. In this daring move, Jesus was claiming to be representing God's people, as the Son of man had done in Daniel's dream. This is particularly striking when we consider the fact that He said this in front of the high priest and the Jerusalem council—the Jewish leaders who saw *themselves* as holding that representative role for the people. Right in their face and right in their headquarters in Jerusalem, Jesus daringly tells them that *He* is now playing that part. *He* is the Son of man, the true representative of God's people. And God would rescue *Him* from His enemies and give *Him* dominion over all the nations. Tough words from a poor defendant on trial, especially from one whose own life was on the line!

But that is not all. If Jesus was claiming to be the persecuted Son of man here in this trial before the chief priests, what was He saying about His accusers? In Jesus' astonishing retelling of this traditional story from Daniel, the leaders of Jerusalem have assumed the role of the beasts who persecute the Son of man. Now *they* are the enemies of the Jews because *they* are opposing the one whom God had sent to free God's people.

Can you feel the punch line? Jesus is saying that the leaders of Jerusalem have become like the Gentile monsters which have oppressed the Jews for centuries. The leaders of God's people have become the enemies of God's people. The chief priests have become the chief beasts.[1] Jesus simply could not have struck a lower blow to His accusers. It's hardly surprising that Caiaphas tore his robe and shouted, "Blasphemy!" while the others beat Him, spat on His face, and called for the death penalty.

Trial Before Pilate

Under Roman rule, the Jews did not have the authority to carry out an execution on their own. That's why the chief priests handed Jesus over to Pilate, the Roman governor who was in charge of Palestine.

---

[1] Chris Wright, *Knowing Jesus Through the Old Testament* (Downers Grove, IL: InterVarsity Press, 1992), 152-53.

The reader of Matthew 27 should notice how Jesus' trial before Pilate is much different from His interrogation before Caiaphas. As the local leader for the Roman empire, Pilate was not concerned about what Jesus thought of the Temple. He was not interested in whether Jesus claimed to be the Son of man in Daniel 7 or what Jesus thought about the chief priests. Pilate basically had only one question for Jesus, and it was a political one: "Are you the King of the Jews?" (Mt. 27:11).

In the Roman world, there is no king but Caesar. Any opposition to Rome must be squashed immediately. Any rival king to the Emperor must be exterminated. So Pilate sought to determine if Jesus really was some type of rebel king, a real threat to the empire.

Pilate soon realized that Jesus was not the ordinary sort of revolutionary leader who threatened Roman rule. He knew that the real issue in Jesus' trial involved a religious rivalry with the Jewish authorities (cf. Mt. 27:18). Pilate wanted to release Jesus, but he could not withstand the pressure from the crowds who had been stirred up by the chief priests and were demanding that Jesus be crucified. John's Gospel tells us that the crowds even threatened Pilate, telling him that if he released a rebel-king, he would prove himself to be a traitorous governor, disloyal to Caesar: "If you release this man, you are not Caesar's friend; every one who makes himself a king sets himself against Caesar" (Jn. 19:12). The last thing Pilate would want would be for that type of accusation to reach Caesar's ears back home in Rome. Afraid of a riot and fearing for his own job, Pilate caved in and handed Jesus over to be crucified (cf. Mt. 27:26).

The Final Choice

In the midst of the mounting riot surrounding the trial, Pilate offered to release one prisoner to the Jews, either Jesus or a man named Barabbas. "Whom do you want me to release for you, Barabbas or Jesus who is called Christ?" (Mt. 27:17). He left it to the crowd to decide, and they chose Barabbas, telling Pilate to send Jesus to the Cross.

Who was this mysterious prisoner named Barabbas? And why would the crowds choose him over Jesus? Barabbas means "son of the father." Besides giving us his name, however, Matthew doesn't say much about him. But he does give us one little description that is quite revealing. He tells us that Barabbas was "a notorious prisoner"—so notorious that Matthew could assume that his readers would have had no doubt which Barabbas he was talking about. It was the famous Barabbas who was imprisoned for murder during a revolt of the revolutionary movement (cf. Mk. 15:7; Lk. 23:19; Jn. 18:40).

So when Pilate stood before the crowds with this offer, the Jews were faced with one final choice: the rebel Barabbas or Jesus. But this wasn't just a choice between two different prisoners. It was a symbolic choice between two different ways of being Israel. Who was the true Israelite? Who was the true son of the Father?

Which road would the people follow? The way of Barabbas or the way of Jesus? The path of bitter nationalism or the path of welcoming in all the outcasts and Gentiles? The way of war, vengeance, and military action, or the way of peace, forgiveness, and the patient enduring of suffering?

Ultimately it came down to choosing between the way of the revolutionary separatists or the way of the Cross. The crowds chose the former, while Jesus went down the latter.

* * *

Questions for Discussion

1. Read Matthew 26:57-68. What were the charges brought against Jesus in His trial before the high priest?

_____

_____

_____

2. Why does the high priest Caiaphas accuse Jesus of blasphemy (Mt. 26:65)? Why are Caiaphas and the chief priests so upset at Jesus' words? To answer these questions, consider the following:

(a) Read Daniel 7:1-18, 24-27. According to Daniel 7:17, who do the beasts represent?

_____

_____

_____

(b) What happens to the "Son of man" figure in this vision? Who is defeated when the Son of man appears?

_____

_____

_____

(c) In light of this Daniel 7 background, what is Jesus saying about *Himself* when He claims to be the "Son of man" in Matthew 26:64?

_____

_____

(d) In light of this Daniel 7 background, what is Jesus saying about *His accusers* when He claims to be the "Son of man"?

_____

3. Read Matthew 27:15-23, Mark 15:7, Luke 23:18-19, and John 18:38-40.

(a) What was Barabbas known for?

_____

_____

(b) What movement in first-century Judaism would Barabbas represent?

_____

_____

(c) From our reflections in this chapter, what is the meaning of the name "Barabbas"?

_____

_____

(d) What is the symbolism of the crowd's choosing Barabbas instead of Jesus?

_____

_____

4. Read Matthew 27:24-26.

(a) Why does Pilate give in to the crowd?

_____

(b) Read John 19:12-16. What do you think Pilate is ultimately afraid of? What might have happened to Pilate if he released Jesus?

_____

_____

_____

5. Like Pilate, we too often let our fears keep us from doing what we know is the right thing to do. Sometimes it is fear of what others may think of us or what they may say about us. Other times it is fear of losing a job, losing someone's respect, or not receiving a promotion. Sometimes it is fear of having to admit that we have failed or done something wrong, or fear of asking someone for their forgiveness.

(a) What fears do you think keep people from doing the right thing? Why is this so?

_____

_____

_____

(b) How is Jesus' embrace of the Cross a model for how we should face the worries and anxieties in our own lives which keep us from being the men and women God wants us to be?

_____

_____

11

THE CLIMAX OF THE CROSS
—MATTHEW 27:27-66—

Roman crucifixion was a horrendous way to die. It didn't just bring a criminal to his death, but it did so with the greatest possible pain and humiliation.

The act itself was not intended to strike at vital organs or cause terminal bleeding. Rather, it was meant to cause a slow and painful death through shock or asphyxiation as the body's breathing muscles gradually collapsed—a process which sometimes took several days.

To inflict maximum humiliation, the condemned person was stripped naked, whipped thirty-nine times, and tied or nailed to a post. Then he was raised up high and ridiculed by those passing by. In the process, the people could see very clearly what would happen to those who dared to resist Roman rule.

All this sent a strong message to people like the Jews who were subject to the domination of the Roman Empire. It said, "We control your entire nation. We can do whatever we want with you. We can even take your body, nail it to a slab of wood, and make you suffer this excruciatingly painful death. Don't even think about rising up against us." This is why the cross would have stood out for the Jews as a somber symbol of their desperate condition and a constant reminder of their subjugation under the Romans.

A Crucified Messiah?

With this background in mind, it is understandable why many Jews in the first century would have been puzzled by a crucified Messiah. They were expecting the Messiah to lead them in triumph over the foreign oppressors and bring freedom to the land. Many would have looked at Jesus dying on the Cross and said, "How could *this* be the Messiah? The Messiah was supposed to *defeat* the Romans, not be defeated *by* them!" Far from appearing as a victorious king, Jesus would have seemed in their eyes to be more like a lost cause—another would-be messiah who let the people down. No wonder some people mocked Him on Calvary, crying out: "If He is the king of Israel, let him come down from the Cross!" (cf. Mt. 27:39-44).

The mystery of the Cross continues to confound people today. If Jesus was the promised Messiah, why did He die such a tragic death? Let's take a look at how Christ's moment of defeat is actually His greatest victory, how His utter debasement stands as His greatest exaltation, and how His death on the Cross actually is His enthronement as Messiah-King. One clue to this mystery of the Cross is found at the Last Supper, where Jesus is portrayed as the new Passover lamb.

A New Passover

The fact that Jesus was handed over and crucified during the time of Passover would have been of great significance to the Jews of His day. This annual celebration was the feast of all feasts which summed up Israel's history and fueled their hopes for a new era that would bring freedom from foreign oppression and forgiveness of Israel's sins.

One reason the Passover was so important is that it recalled the fateful night when God freed Israel from slavery in Egypt during the time of Moses. Despite several plagues which fell on the Egyptians, Pharaoh repeatedly refused to let the Israelites go. But on the night of that first Passover, God instructed the Israelites to slay an unblemished lamb, eat its flesh, and mark their door posts with the lamb's blood. Then all the first-born sons in Egypt were struck down that night, while the Israelite first-born sons were spared because Yahweh "passed over" the homes which had the mark of the lamb's blood (Ex. 12). After this tenth and most severe plague, Pharaoh finally released the Israelites from slavery, and the people fled Egypt in the night. Thus, that first Passover brought about Israel's redemption from slavery and their national identity as God's chosen people.

Subsequent generations of Israelites remembered this foundational event by celebrating the Passover feast. Once a year, they sacrificed a lamb and ate it in this sacred meal in order to symbolize their solidarity with their deceased ancestors from the first Passover in the Exodus.

Another reason the Passover was so important was that it not only looked to the past, but also turned to the future as Jews would plea for Yahweh to vindicate His people once again. Especially in the time of Jesus, the Passover was associated with great messianic expectation and hope for a *new* exodus. What God did for Israel through Moses, He would do again through the Messiah. What God did to Pharaoh and the Egyptians, He would do again to Pilate and the Romans. And many Jews believed God would bring about this new exodus once again on the day of the Passover. In fact, an ancient Passover poem used in synagogue liturgy depicts four great events in salvation history occurring on the same calendar day as the Passover feast: creation of the universe, the covenant with Abraham, and Israel's deliverance from Egypt all occurred on the night of the Passover. And according to this poem, it was on this same night that the future messianic king was expected to bring redemption to the Jews.[1]

Imagine the messianic anticipation that must have filled the hearts of the disciples when Jesus instructed them to prepare the Passover meal. This must have been the capstone in a week of mounting expectations. Earlier that week, the disciples had watched their Master enter the Davidic city of Jerusalem in royal fashion riding on a donkey. They witnessed how the crowds claimed Him as a king. They saw Him cleanse the Temple as Israel's kings had done. And now, with Passover just around the corner—and all the messianic hopes bound up with this feast— some of the disciples preparing the Passover meal were probably wondering if this was the night when Jesus would carry out His messianic work: "Could this be *the* Passover that we've all been waiting for? Could this be the Passover night when the Messiah would enact the new exodus and rescue our people?"

---

[1] This poem, called the "Poem of the Four Nights," is found in the Targum *Neophyti*, an Aramaic paraphrase of the Old Testament used for synagogue worship. See *Neophyti* I, vol. 2 (Madrid-Barcelona, 1970), 312-13, as cited in Lucien Deiss, *It's the Lord's Supper* (London: Collins, 1975), 35.

The Lamb of God

What is most striking about the account of the Last Supper is that the Passover lamb is nowhere mentioned in the entire narrative. The eating of the lamb came at the climax of the Passover feast. But just at the moment when one would expect the lamb to be eaten, Jesus did something rather surprising:

> Jesus took bread, and blessed, and broke it, and gave it to the disciples and said "Take, eat; this is my body." And he took a cup, and when he had given thanks he gave it to them, saying, "Drink of it, all of you; for this is my blood of the covenant, which is poured out for many for the forgiveness of sins" (Mt. 26:26-28).

Instead of the Passover lamb, Jesus spoke of *His* own body being eaten. Instead of the lamb's sacrificial blood, Jesus spoke of *His* own blood being poured out in sacrifice. In this meal, Jesus dramatically pre-enacted what would take place on Good Friday. The breaking of bread symbolized how Jesus' own body soon would be broken on the Cross. The cup of blood being poured out symbolized how His own blood soon would be poured out on Calvary. Jesus was symbolically saying that He was like the Passover lamb. Just as the Passover lamb was offered up in sacrifice in order to free the Israelite first-born sons in Egypt, Jesus will be offered in order to free God's first-born son, the nation of Israel (cf. Ex. 4:22).

State of the Nation

Another window into the mystery of the Cross is found in Jesus' mission as Israel's representative

Messiah-King. Recall how in chapter three we saw that the Jews viewed their king as standing in the place of the entire nation. He was Israel's royal representative, summing up the entire people in himself, so much so that what happened to the king would be understood as having happened to the people as a whole. Now we will see how Jesus, assuming that role as messianic representative, will bring Israel's history to its climax on the Cross and carry the people to their ultimate destiny. To do this, we must first look at one element from Israel's tradition which probably shaped the way the Jews looked at their own tragic history and hoped for Israel's restoration more than anything else: the solemn covenant Israel entered into with Yahweh in the Book of Deuteronomy.

This foundational covenant, made just before the people entered the Promised Land, put before the Israelites two paths which would set the course of their history all the way up to the time of Jesus. One path was the way of faithfulness and covenant blessing, while the other was the way of unfaithfulness and destruction. Moses told the people that if they remained faithful to Yahweh, they would be blessed in the Promised Land. But if they proved unfaithful to Yahweh, they would close themselves off from God's blessings and a series of curses would fall upon them. Fevers, illnesses, blindness, and leprosy would ravage the people. Famine, drought, and pestilence would cover the land. Foreign armies would constantly attack their nation.

The ultimate curse, however, was exile: Pagan empires would drive the Israelites out from the Promised Land and carry them away as slaves. Even their king would be handed over to the Gentiles, and Israel would be completely destroyed. With all this turmoil thrown onto Israel, it is no wonder that Moses described the horrors of the curses as a type of covenant death: "I call heaven and earth to witness against you this day, that I have set before you life and death, blessing and curse; therefore choose life, that you and your descendants may live." (Deut. 30:19).

Unfortunately, Israel did not choose the way of covenant faithfulness. In rejecting the God who wanted to bless them, Israel knew that it had suffered the painful effects of life outside the blessing, just as Deuteronomy had foretold. As the prophet Daniel explained, this was the background for understanding Israel's sad state of affairs under foreign oppression: "[T]he curse and oath which are written in the law of Moses the servant of God have been poured out upon us, because we have sinned" (Dan. 9:11).

Friends in Low Places

How did Christ's death on the Cross free Israel from this mess? Sometimes, Jesus' work of redemption is presented as if He simply stepped in and took our punishment by being crucified. In this perspective, Jesus was an innocent victim who took our penalty for us, freeing us from the divine wrath which we, as sinners, truly deserved.

The Scriptures, however, tell us there is something more to the mystery of the Cross. As the people's messianic representative, Jesus did not die simply as a substitute for Israel, but in solidarity with Israel, especially in its lowest points. Throughout His ministry,

Jesus went out to the darkest corners of the nation to meet the people in the places where the suffering was most acute and the powers of evil ran most rampant. He reached out to the blind and the lame. He touched the untouchable lepers and dead bodies. He entered into intimate table fellowship with some of the most renowned sinners. And He even approached demoniacs to free them from the power of Satan.

Every step of the way, Jesus identified Himself with the sinners and outcasts who were considered ritually impure and estranged from the covenant. Yet, instead of being defiled by them, Jesus' holiness overpowered their impurities, bringing physical healing and covenant restoration. In this way, Jesus met the people of Israel in the valley of their suffering and sin in order to unite Himself to them in their dismal condition and lift them up to blessing and new life.

All this came to a climax on the Cross. There, Jesus plunged into the depths of Israel's agony. As Israel's representative Messiah-King, He entered into the people's intense suffering under foreign oppression as He Himself was taken away and crucified by the Gentile enemies. And there on the Cross, Jesus took the ultimate step of meeting Israel at its lowest point of all—its state of covenant death. In uniting Himself to Israel in its estrangement from God and in its covenantal death as a nation, Jesus could lift the people out of the grave in the Resurrection. In joining Himself to the depths of Israel's sufferings on Good Friday, He could raise them up with Him on Easter Sunday. This was the real victory of the Messiah. Indeed, He truly set the people free, just as the prophets had foretold, but not in the way many expected. It was not a triumph over Caesar, Herod, and the Roman empire, but a victory over the real enemies of the Jews: sin, death, and the forces of evil. It was a battle won not by swords and soldiers, but by the patient enduring of suffering and the radical outpouring of love and forgiveness. It was not an end of the geographical exile in being separated from control over their land, but the end of Israel's deeper, spiritual exile in being separated from God.

Adam's Family

Israel, however, was not the only nation that Jesus came to rescue. *All* the children of Adam suffered from a life estranged from God and cut off from His blessing. All humanity stood in need of Christ's Redemption. This is seen in the story of the human family's first father, Adam.

Genesis 3 describes how Adam was tested by the serpent in the Garden of Eden, and he broke covenant with God by eating from the forbidden tree. As a result, Adam faced several curses. His work would not be easy as it was in paradise. Now he would have to labor "in the sweat" (Gen. 3:19) while his harvest would yield "thorns and thistles" (Gen. 3:18). Even the ground on which he worked would be cursed (Gen. 3:17). The ultimate curse, however, was death, when Adam would return to the ground at the end of his life: "for out of it you were taken; you are dust, and to dust you shall return" (Gen. 3:19).

In His Passion and death, Jesus entered into the curses of Adam which had plagued humanity since the time of the Fall. Just as He did for Israel, Jesus also united Himself to the sufferings and curses of all the children of Adam. Like Adam, Jesus was tested in a garden—the Garden of Gethsemane—the night before He died (Mt. 26:36-46). There, He took on Adam's sweat, as His "sweat became like great drops of blood" falling from His face (Lk. 22:44). And He took on Adam's thorns as the Roman soldiers mockingly placed a crown of thorns upon His head (Mt. 27:29). Finally, Jesus even entered into Adam's death by going to "a tree" (Gal. 3:13)—the wood of the Cross—and dying on Calvary. And like Adam, Jesus went down to the ground where He was buried— and it was precisely by meeting humanity at that despairingly darkest point that He could lift Adam and the human race out of the grave with Him in His victory over all sin and death on Easter morning (Mt. 27:59-61; 28:1-10).[2] As the New Adam, Jesus has redeemed not just Israel, but the entire human race (Rom. 5:12-21).

Faith of Our Fathers

Let us consider one final perspective which may shed light on the mystery of the Cross: Jesus' sacrifice as the fulfillment of the covenant promise God made to Abraham.

In the later years of Abraham's life, God put the patriarch's faith to a most severe test. One day He said to Abraham, "Take your son, your only son

---

[2] On the Adam-Christ parallels, see Scott Hahn, *A Father Who Keeps His Promises* (Ann Arbor: Servant Publications, 1998), 63-76.

Isaac, whom you love, and go to the land of Moriah, and offer him there as a burnt offering upon one of the mountains of which I shall tell you" (Gen. 22:2). Abraham rose early the next morning, cut the wood for the offering, saddled his donkey, and traveled with his son to Moriah just as God had instructed. When they arrived, they ascended the mountain with Isaac carrying the wood for the sacrifice on his shoulders. After reaching the top, Abraham prepared the altar for the sacrifice and then bound his son and placed him on the wood. The sacrifice was ready to begin.

> Then Abraham put forth his hand, and took the knife to slay his son. But the angel of the LORD called to him from heaven, and said, "Abraham, Abraham! . . . Do not lay your hand on the lad or do anything to him; for now I know that you fear God, seeing you have not withheld your son, your only son, from me" (Gen. 22:10-12).

The story ends with God rewarding Abraham with a most amazing promise. Because Abraham was willing to give God everything, God swore a covenant oath that Abraham's family would have the privileged role of being God's chosen people to bless the world. Through Abraham's descendants, the nations would find God's blessing.

> By myself I have sworn . . . because you have done this, and have not withheld your son, your only son, I will indeed bless you, and I will multiply your descendants . . . and by your descendants shall all the nations of the earth bless themselves, because you have obeyed my voice (Gen. 22:16-18).

Worldwide Blessing

Most commentators on this passage discuss the great faith of Abraham. Few, however, ponder the incredible faith Isaac must have had. Imagine what Isaac was feeling when he saw his own dad tie him up, put him on the altar, and bring out a knife to slay him! One interesting note about this narrative is that Isaac may have been in his teens at this time. He certainly was old enough to carry the wood and to understand the ritual procedures for the sacrifice (Gen. 22:7). Thus, he probably was old enough to run away or resist his elderly father, who was over one hundred years old at the time.[3] Such a view would fit with what the ancient Jewish rabbis and some early Christians took for granted: that Isaac was a voluntary victim who willingly submitted to being offered in obedience to God's command. If this perspective is correct, Isaac freely chose to go along with God's plan, even if it meant his own death.[4] Now that's faith!

This suspenseful story about Abraham and Isaac, however, is much more than a tale of great faith. It is also a ritually enacted statement about how God would accomplish His plan of salvation for all humanity. In fact, if we look a little closer at this story, we will see that the offering of Isaac on Moriah prefigures what

---

[3] G. Wenham, *Genesis 16-50* (Waco, TX: Word, 1987), 115: "The Old Testament nowhere speaks of sacrificial animals having their legs bound before slaughter, and if Isaac had been reluctant to be sacrificed, it would have been easier for Abraham to have cut his throat or stabbed him rather than tie him up first and then place him on the altar. But he was tied, indicating his own willing submission to God's command revealed to his father." See also Scott Hahn, *Kinship by Covenant* (Ann Arbor: UMI Dissertation Services, 1995), 194-95.
[4] *Ibid.*

will actually happen to Jesus in the very same place some two thousand years later.

Mount Moriah wasn't just any ordinary mountain in the desert. It was the sacred place which later came to be known as Jerusalem (cf. 2 Chron. 3:1; Ps. 76:1-3). With this background, we can see that just as Abraham offered his only-beloved son, Isaac, on Mount Moriah, so did Our Heavenly Father offer His only beloved Son on Calvary—which happens to be one of the hills of Moriah.[5] Like Isaac, who journeyed to Mount Moriah with a donkey, Jesus traveled up that same mountain in a similar way on Palm Sunday, entering the holy city of Jerusalem riding on a young donkey. And on His way up to Calvary on Good Friday, Jesus shouldered the wood for the sacrifice—the wood of the Cross—just as Isaac had carried the sacrificial wood up the mountain for his father's offering.

And when Jesus arrived at Calvary—broken, beaten, and barely walking—He willingly stretched out His hands and laid His body on the wood, allowing Himself to be bound to the Cross and offered as a voluntary sacrifice—reminiscent of Isaac's free offering of himself on that same mountain. This time, however, there was no angel to stop the sacrifice, for the Son was determined to offer Himself like a lamb on our behalf. And He did all this in order to bring about the world-wide blessing which God—right there on Moriah—swore He would carry out through Abraham's children. Indeed, Jesus was that faithful

---

[5] Hahn, *A Father Who Keeps His Promises*, 108.

"son of Abraham" (Mt. 1:1), that faithful Israelite, through whom a broken human family would find healing and reunion with its heavenly Father. In this way, Israel's mission to the nations was finally accomplished. Through Jesus, God's blessing went out from Israel to embrace the whole world. Through its messianic representative and His work on the Cross, Israel finally became what it was always meant to be: light to the world. And Israel's light never shined brighter than when it pierced the tomb on Easter morning and overpowered the darkness which covered the face of the earth.

*   *   *

Questions for Discussion

1. From our reflections in this chapter, what would Roman crucifixion have symbolized for the Jews living under Caesar's domination?

_____

_____

_____

2. In light of this, why would the Crucifixion of Jesus be such an obstacle to the Jews' accepting Him as their Messiah-King?

_____

_____

3. How do you think Matthew's Gospel helps remove that obstacle and show that Jesus' death on the Cross really is His moment of triumph as the Messiah-King?

_____

_____

_____

4. Read Matthew 26:17-29.

(a) How does Jesus associate Himself with the Passover lamb at the Last Supper?

_____

_____

(b) How does this shed light on Jesus' sacrifice on the Cross on Good Friday?

_____

_____

5. Read Genesis 3:17-19.

(a) List the punishments given to Adam for his sin in these verses.

_____

_____

(b) How does Jesus take on these punishments of Adam in His Passion and death?

_____

_____

6. Read the dramatic story of Abraham and Isaac in Genesis 22:1-18.

(a) Who did God ask Abraham to offer in sacrifice in verse 2?

_____

_____

(b) Where does God instruct them to go in verse 2?

_____

_____

(c) From the reflections in this chapter, what city is later built on this spot?

_____

_____

(d) What animal do they take with them for their travel in verse 3?

_____

_____

(e) What does Isaac carry up the mountain?

_____

_____

(f) How did Jewish tradition interpret Isaac's participation in this sacrifice?

_____

_____

(g) As a result of Abraham's great faith, what did God promise He was going to bring about through Abraham's descendants in verse 18?

_____

_____

7. In what ways does this story of Abraham and Isaac prefigure what God the Father and His Son Jesus will do on the Cross?

_____

_____

_____

CONCLUSION
—MATTHEW 28—

"All authority in heaven and on earth has been given to me. Go therefore and make disciples of all nations, baptizing them in the name of the Father and of the Son and of the Holy Spirit, teaching them to observe all that I have commanded you; and lo, I am with you always, to the close of the age" (Mt. 28:18-20).

With these words of Jesus, Saint Matthew brings his Gospel to a triumphant close, proclaiming the victory of the Messiah and the splendor of His worldwide kingdom.

In this passage, Jesus approaches the apostles for the first time since His Resurrection. When they see their risen Messiah, they worship Him as He solemnly declares to them something He never explicitly proclaimed before: "All authority in heaven and on earth has been given to me" (Mt. 28:18).

These words tie together one of the most important themes in Matthew's Gospel: Jesus' authority as the Messiah. Throughout the Gospel, Matthew has been preparing His readers for understanding Jesus' full authority as the victorious Messiah-King. In the opening chapter, Jesus is introduced in the genealogy with kingly authority as the climactic Son of David coming at the end of the royal Davidic line. At the start of His public life, Jesus manifested His power over Israel's greatest enemy, the devil, as He withstood the three temptations in the desert. Throughout His ministry, Jesus proved Himself to be a teacher with great

authority (7:28-29), and His powerful actions of healing the sick, forgiving sins, and exorcising demons
demonstrated His authority over all physical ailments, over sin, and even over evil spirits (cf. 9:33).
All this, however, was but a prelude to the ultimate
manifestation of Jesus' supreme authority which
came in His Crucifixion on Good Friday and in His
Resurrection on Easter Sunday. Only after defeating
the real enemies of God's people—sin and death—in
His Resurrection does Jesus make this triumphant
declaration to His apostles: "All authority in heaven
and on earth has been given to me."

Here, Daniel's image of the "Son of man" will come
in handy again. Recall how in Daniel's vision the Son
of man figure represented God's people as they were
trampled over by the four great kingdoms symbolized
by the four fierce beasts (cf. Dan. 7:23-27). But then,
rather surprisingly, the Son of man was rescued by
God, and in the end he rises victorious over the enemies of God's people and is given *authority* to rule
over all the earth.

Like the mysterious figure in Daniel, Jesus also
shared the suffering of God's people. There on the
Cross, Jesus experienced firsthand the beasts swarm-
ing around Him in full force, as the enemies of God's
people persecuted Him and brought Him to His tragic death. But this wasn't the end of the story. Just as
God delivered the Son of man from the evil powers, so
did God rescue Jesus in His darkest hour, raising Him
from the tomb on Easter morning. Only now, as the
Son of man vindicated and victorious, does Jesus pro-
claim His dominion over all things, saying to the
apostles: "All authority in heaven and on earth has

been given to me." The story of Daniel 7 had been brought to its fulfillment in Christ's Resurrection.

Now it was up to the apostles to continue Christ's mission by bringing His kingdom to the whole world. This is why Jesus commissions the apostles to go out to all the earth teaching and baptizing all peoples:

> Go therefore and make disciples of all nations, baptizing them in the name of the Father and of the Son and of the Holy Spirit, teaching them to observe all that I have commanded you (Mt. 28:19 20).

Recall how in Matthew 10 Jesus already bestowed upon the apostles His very authority to announce the kingdom in His name by preaching and healing just as He had done (Mt. 10:1-15). In that first commissioning, however, Jesus sent them out only to "the lost sheep of the house of Israel" (Mt. 10:6). But now after Christ's death and Resurrection, the kingdom bursts out across all borders. Now that the Messiah-King has freed God's people from their true oppressors, light can finally pour forth from Israel to all the nations. As the Jewish people's royal representative, Jesus will finally accomplish what Israel was always meant to do: bring all nations back into union with the one true God. And He will do that through His apostles. Invested with the authority of the Messiah-King Himself, the apostles are commissioned to gather all nations into Christ's kingdom and carry out His triumph over sin and death in the lives of people all over the world.

They won't be alone in that mission. Jesus promises to *be with* the apostles until the end of time. Here Matthew's Gospel ends in the same place it

began: with the theme of Emmanuel. We saw earlier
how the first chapter of the Gospel culminated with
Jesus' receiving the glorious title "Emmanuel,"
meaning *God with us* (Mt. 1:23). Now, twenty-seven
chapters later, at the close of the Gospel, Emmanuel
Himself promises to "*be with*" the apostles in their
mission of bringing the kingdom to all the nations.

And like the apostles, we won't be alone in our
mission. The same Jesus who promised to be with
the apostles two thousand years ago continues to be
with us as we help build Christ's kingdom in the
world today. He promises to be with us when we
pray, especially whenever two or three are gathered
in His name (Mt. 18:20). He is with us in the inspired
words of the Scriptures, through which God speaks
lovingly to us as His children (cf. Catechism, nos. 80,
104). He is with us in the Church through the bishops,
who serve as the apostles' successors and Christ's
representatives in their shepherding and teaching
of the Christian people (cf. Catechism, no. 860).
And most intimately, Jesus remains with us in His
Real Presence in the Holy Eucharist, which fills us
with His very life during our journey here on earth
(cf. Catechism, nos. 1373-81). Confident in Jesus'
presence with us, we are now called to go forward
and bring the kingdom of Christ to a broken, wounded
world that is longing for the healing, freedom, and
love that only Christ can give.